WHY HISTORY?

D1448602

Marjorie Reeves

WHY HISTORY?

LONGMAN

LONGMAN GROUP LIMITED
London
Associated companies, branches and representatives
throughout the world

© Longman Group Ltd. 1980

First published 1980
ISBN 0 582 36119 2 cased
     0 582 36120 6 paper

Set in 10/11 VIP Baskerville
by Herts Typesetting Services Ltd.

Printed in Great Britain
by Richard Clay and Company Limited, Bungay

British Library Cataloguing in Publication Data

Reeves, Marjorie
   Why History?
   1. History – Study and teaching
   I. Title
   907'.1   L131581

   ISBN 0-582-36119-2
   ISBN 0-582-36120-6 Pbk

Contents

Preface

Many children and teachers have contributed ingredients for this book, although for the mixing and the baking of the cake I alone must take responsibility. I owe a particular debt to two people. Mrs. Margaret Walsh Wheeler has immensely enlarged my understanding and vision of education, besides providing me with some precious illustrative material. Mr. William K. Ritchie has very kindly prepared the bibliographies to the topics in Chapter 8. In expressing my gratitude to them I must at the same time release them from any obligation to approve of the opinions and judgements expressed in this book.

Marjorie E. Reeves

1
A love affair with history

History can be at once the most repelling, mystifying and attracting subject in the curriculum. Those present participles endow the subject with power, almost personifying it, as Dante, when he discovered philosophy, celebrated the beauties of the Lady Philosophy in the style of the troubadours. I shall not write of the eyes and the smile of the Lady History, but the personification metaphor for a brief moment serves a purpose. Learning involves a relationship. This may be a strictly limited, utilitarian relationship, as when we seek to acquire a skill or information which we propose to use for purposes beyond itself, for our own ends. This is analogous to acquiring a tool across the counter, and is certainly not to be despised in a world where knowledge is needed for the service of men. But 'personal knowledge' begins with an involvement that is like the developing relationship with another person. It starts with the desire to explore the barely glimpsed unknown 'personality'; it becomes a commitment that engages the imagination as well as the intellect; it develops into a conviction that here is something worth knowing for its own sake. The experience becomes a kind of love affair which is both subjective in origin and objective in intention. You engage in it in order to enjoy – what? The personification metaphor is almost irresistible in describing this relationship. The historian who wrote in his preface: 'I apologise to my wife for the love affair I have had with my subject' expressed the matter very neatly.

But the Lady History certainly assumes many shapes in school. She can take on the most ugly form. The common reply in discovering that one teaches history is: 'Oh, I hated it at school – all dates and battles!' This is the memory of a frustrating experience – wanting to relate oneself and being repelled, because there seemed to be nothing intelligible to latch on to. Then she can take the mystifying shape of something which might be attractive but seems to have no point. 'What's it for?' is the question.[1] Almost any other subject is easier to

[1] Marc Bloch starts his last (unfinished) book, *The Historian's Craft*, with his son's question: 'Tell me, Daddy. What is the use of history?' (Manchester University Press, 1954, p. 3).

explain in terms either of utility or personal experience. Yet history's attractions remain: historical novels, plays, films, and television history shows do not lose their appeal; digging up the past is a popular holiday activity; collecting the past as a hobby now extends to old gas lamps and the oddest bric-a-brac. Adults who gladly escaped from her embrace at school return later to pursue her charms.

The fundamental problem is that we are not sure what kind of a study this is intended to be. If it has no immediate practical use, of what value is it as an experience? It does not give us skills to compute our way through life, nor does it in any obvious sense explain our often confusing experience. It cannot fend off that great cultural shock of our age: rapid social change. That shock, says Alvin Toffler, forces us into the future, and what can history safely tell us about the future? Yet past generations thought they knew what history was for. The hey-day of history in education probably began with our great-great grandfathers, who were clear enough about its importance. History was full of moral lessons which shaded from noble heroics to awful warnings. So there appeared a flood of little books with prefaces that urged the young aspirants on the upward way and vivid black-and-white pictures to dramatise the acts of history. It gave a satisfying sense of control over life to be able to wrap up the characters of kings in succinct moral judgements, as thus: 'George II was choleric – but neither vindictive, nor malignant: he was brave, determined and intriguing.'[1] The famous Mrs. Trimmer could allow herself to be severe on Queen Elizabeth I. Whilst praising her statesmanship she pronounces: 'She was subject to passions which led her into actions that reflect great discredit on her memory.'[2] J. Newbery, the eighteenth-century children's friend, had already stated the objective of history when he said that he wanted his readers to be made wise and happy from the example of others which is the true use and end of history.[3] It was in this spirit that *The British Nepos or Mirror of Youth*[4] offered 'Select Lives of Illustrious Britons who have distinguished themselves by their virtues, talents or remarkable advancement in life.' Its frontispiece shows 'The Genius of Biography' directing 'British Youth' to the Temple of Honour by the path of Industry and Perseverance. The two eager scholars at the foot of the path have to climb from Alfred the Great to John Howard before achieving the temple on the top. In such books the assumptions

---

[1] Riley's *Biographical and Chronological Tablet of English History*.
[2] *A Description of a Set of Prints of English History*, Pt. II.
[3] *A Compendious History of the World compiled for the use of Young Gentlemen and Ladies by their Old Friend Mr. Newbery*, 1763.
[4] By William Mavor, second edition, 1800.

were that moral values were unchanging and that each generation learnt by simple imitation. The correlations seemed obvious.

As doubts began to be cast on the reality of this beautiful equation between past and present experience, more sophisticated variants were brought to the defence of history. Nations – if not individuals – could learn from the mistakes of history; its lessons were still directly valid in terms of practical consequences, if not moral values. There was often a hint of a cyclical view in the argument that history repeats itself and therefore a people can be forewarned. There is just enough shred of truth in this belief for it to linger with us still, as witness the parallel between the tragedies of Napoleon's and Hitler's Russian expeditions. But in general this argument for history has long since been exploded. History never really repeats itself. Indeed, it can sometimes assume the shape of a false siren, luring on to the rocks people who engage in fighting yesterday's battles rather than those of today, repeating yesterday's mistakes rather than correcting them.

Bit by bit theories of the moral value or usefulness of historical 'lessons' have been worn away, until the factor of accelerated change has provided a logic which seems to dispose of most history as utterly irrelevant. One of the rising generation said to me: 'With change proceeding in a nightmare geometrical progression, of what use to me is the experience of people born before the Second World War?' And another said: 'How can anything before the Space Age teach me to cope with it?' So the Lady History is pushed firmly out of the back door. If she is to have a place at all at our banquet of good learning, she will have to re-enter at the front door, that is, she will have to be entertained in her own right, because we want her for herself. But the prospect looks bleak. Watching the direction of their curiosities, it sometimes seems to me that for many children today the experience of time does not come as naturally as the experience of space. Space is a part of everyday life and the phenomenal growth of communications brings it all the more dramatically into a child's early experience. He watches space unroll from the car-seat; aeroplanes winging through the sky to Tokyo or Timbuctoo are a sight he understands (partially, at least) as soon as he can ask questions; Space Men are his close acquaintances on television. But if adults make no special effort to introduce the dimension of time, how many children begin spontaneously to ask the historical questions, for example: Who lived in our house before we did? Who first thought of making a fire? How did things begin? Perhaps the continuity of the family gives the most natural introduction to time and history. 'Grannie, what did you do when you were a little girl?' asked a little girl of six. The result was a flood of reminiscences which led to the announcement at school: 'My Grannie says that when she was a little girl *her* Grannie used to tell her when *she* was a girl she had to go to work behind those old iron gates down the road.' And this was the start of a project on Victorian children. Such 'ways in' to the past are eagerly used by many teachers. But with modern family mobility, how many children have grandparents to hand for asking such questions?

The study of space is natural. It begins with the immediate environment and the use of our own legs. It is no accident that 'environmental studies' or 'social studies' have been replacing the traditional history and geography, and that local history often forms part of the history syllabus in both primary and early secondary years. In many ways these new approaches engage the pupil's, imagination, but the result can be that the experience of the past – history – is swamped in this focus on the here and now scene looking forward into the future, which is a different time dimension. Is this intentional? Are we making what may be a profound cultural switch? I doubt it. The case for history is more likely to go by default. It could become just the romantic frilling of society, stuck on by film and television, while the rising generation is studying the mechanisms and mutations of societies. 'What I want to know is what makes *my* world tick,' said a student. The implied image of the machine in this remark is indicative of a significant trend which gathered momentum in the United States and then in Britain over a considerable period: the belief that the predicaments of human living can only be solved by the *sciences* of society. Here we reach a question crucial for the life of future generations. Crudely speaking, the difference between sociology and history is that the one studies the laws of human social behaviour, drawing out general principles from a mass of particular data, while the other studies the uniqueness of human actions in all their particularity. Of course one shades into the other in social and economic history, but there is a fundamental difference of approach. The thrill of history is, as Leibniz put it, 'the thrill of learning singular things'. But the attempt of the historian to recapture uniqueness can be the 'scandal of particularity' to the scientific student of societies.

Thus the question for us is whether we believe the human studies we plan for the rising generation should be chiefly centred on societies and their operations or on people and their activities. What are the necessary ingredients in education which will, we hope, make for the 'good life' of the future? Certainly sociology has illuminated human behaviour in a thousand ways and a more scientifically grounded awareness of what is happening to us in our environment can be the fruit of its new insights. But already belief in sociology as providing all the answers is waning and the present vogue of social studies in schools may even now be growing out of date. This book is not an attack on social studies in education, but I do want to press the question: How far can a full human awareness be nourished on the abstracted general statements which are the fruits of sociological study? Do these generalities fire the imagination in the way that the particularities of history do? In 1939–40 not long before he went back to France for the last time Marc Bloch, the great French historian, said in a conversation with Lewis Namier: 'The study of societies and sociology will take the place of history, and we do this at our peril because history will fall into disrepute.'[1] A leading sociologist stated at a conference of the Royal Historical Society in 1970 that he saw 'a long-term cultural process by which history is being superseded by sociology. Historians themselves begin to write of the contemporary waning of the past.'[2] That was in 1970 and there are indications now that these prophecies are not so certain of fulfilment. It is significant that, as far as school education goes, for more than a decade now a search for new themes in history and new approaches to old ones has been going on, producing a flood of fresh material, often inventive, but often fumbling in purpose and method because the real Lady History remains so elusive. And for this and a variety of other causes it still seems that the historical experience is in danger of getting crowded out by more immediately attractive and useful elements in the curriculum. Is that cost too great?

The argument of this book is that such a cost would be too great, but that we have to be clear why the experience of history is an essential element in the nourishment of the next generation before we can devise the approaches and methods through which we can initiate the young into it. An experience it must be – not a collection of facts picked up like pebbles on the sea-shore. Years ago I found myself using this word 'experience' to describe what I felt should be happening in the classroom. It was, I think, a reaction against 'pebble history'. Recently, in 1977, Sir Richard Southern entitled his Rede Lecture in Cambridge 'The Historical Experience'. In it he recounted his own first remembered experience of history:

I was fifteen. Like thousands of our young every year I was facing the depressing prospect of writing an essay on King Henry VII. Acres of facts of intolerable dreariness and frightening unintelligibility stretched out in all directions, numbing the senses. Then suddenly, out of nowhere, the precious words formed themselves in my mind. I can see them yet. They

[1] In a conversation reported to me by Mrs M. W. Wheeler. Marc Bloch was shot for his part in the French Resistance Movement on 16 June 1944.
[2] B. R. Wilson, 'Sociological Methods in the Study of History', *TRHS*, p. 107, 1971.

were: 'Henry VII was the first King of England who was a business man.'
. . . Tracks appeared in the jungle; it was possible to advance. . . . Crude
and naïve though it was, it was a historical experience as genuine as any I
have ever had.[1]

Southern analyses the two essentials of this 'experience' as an initial
perception which was 'sharp and vivid', and an 'urgency of personal
significance'. In this particular case the words 'business man' had
latched on to 'a large body of experience of daily life in a northern
industrial town' and to 'the sound of voices discussing the intricacies
of a family business far into the night'. The essence of 'experience' in
this context is thus seen to lie in a relationship which links something
new and strange in the past with something familiar and understood
in our own lives. It engages the whole personality in a kind of dialogue
with the past which shows us more clearly who we are. The invitation
to history is, indeed, an invitation to a variety of personal
relationships. We must understand and share in these for ourselves
before we can teach history.

But the words 'teach history' are misleading because they appear to
draw a ring round a self-contained subject. On the contrary, the
'historical element' in education is all-pervasive and all-attracting:
wherever there is a history – of number or of science, of literature or
the other arts, of religion, politics or society – there is a place for
historical experience; wherever there is a skill – in mathematics or
geometry, in writing, in art, music or dance – the understanding and
communication of history calls it into service. History can be *par
excellence* a focal point in a programme of integrated studies. The
important thing is to preserve the 'experience of history' rather than
the 'subject of history'.

[1] R. W. Southern, 'The Historical Experience', *TLS*, 24 June, p. 771, 1977.

2

Standing in our own shoes

We belong before we know who we are. History was the godmother at our birth, for the ineluctable fact about human-beings is that they must have a history. The great question is whether she is seen as the good or bad fairy. Does our history help or hamper us? World forces have wrenched millions away from their history and many more abandon it willingly, prizing mobility above all else. I once had a heated argument with a Jewish Rabbi who, in reply to my statement that the initial condition needed in the nurture of children was the security of belonging, argued fiercely that Jewish children had had to be prepared to be torn up and flung into an alien, chaotic world. But the striking fact about the Jewish people is that through long generations they have carried their history with them into the many hostile environments they have encountered. Few societies have been more closely knit than the traditional Jewish family, and this is surely one reason for their amazing resilience. A sense of belonging to a society which was there before you were and which surrounds and over-arches your personal experience is a primary 'food' in the nourishment of the human young. The psychological deprivation of refugee or stray, rootless children is not as apparent as physical starvation but we surely know it. Experts in child care have realised that establishing some link with the past – even a photograph of a parent or a child's original home – can help a waif, cast up by this eddying society of ours, in the process of self- identification. But if the history is a bad one, a 'damnable inheritance', what then? Is it still not better to know your past and, coming to terms with it, go forward more freely? Whatever the special problems of those maladjusted to their past – and they are, alas, too many – the general situation is that in a school we meet a group of, say, thirty or more children, each with his or her own history, each growing out of a state of belonging into one of self-awareness. How do we best foster this process of moving from security to freedom?

It will be obvious that I have been using 'history' in particular senses. In our context I would define it, not as what happened in the past, but, in the first place, as what has survived into the present, whether in deliberately preserved material or by chance, and is therefore available to be remembered, and, secondly, as what out of this surviving past is actually appropriated in the memory of the living and re-created in their imaginations. What concerns us particularly at the moment is memory: individual memory, family memory, group memory. How necessary is this to human living? Is it really a form of deprivation to live two-dimensionally instead of three-dimensionally? Some of the young take a strong position against this third dimension of memory, arguing that history can fetter, and that the 'existentialist position' of finding your identity through the immediacy of present living gives the only true freedom. Yet other people are clearly developing a sense of deprivation, even if their quest for history takes a nostalgic form. It is surely significant that, at this moment when the 'death of history' had been announced, societies for the study of family genealogy and history should be springing up in profusion and people awakening to the importance of old letters, photographs and picture postcards. Old boxes and bottles, domestic utensils, family odds and ends are collected with loving care, and museums put on displays of domestic flotsam and jetsam that they would not have touched fifty years ago. Indeed, a crop of new small museums is springing up, focused on local craft, industry and social life. In the ordering of present personal experience we need, as I have said, the framework of past human living – a structure into which we fit. So we seek to establish a stable picture of what life was like two or three generations ago. Perhaps, rather wistfully, we envisage this as much more secure and unchanging than it really was, but deeper than any nostalgic feeling lies the sense that their way of living is part of ourselves: they are not just 'quaint', but people who belong to us. Perhaps this pursuit of family history has been characteristically a middle-class taste but two of the classics which bring family memory to life – Flora Thompson's *Lark Rise to Candleford* and M. K. Ashby's *Joseph Ashby of Tysoe* – have a quite humble background. A very noticeable phenomenon is the variety of the people who enjoy exhibitions of past social life, poring over ancient spectacles, early cameras and old doll's houses, exploring the reconstructed kitchen or smithy, being photographed in a vintage motor car or working the ancient fire-engine, as I saw in a Toronto museum. An exhibition of Byegones in a Wiltshire village produced an astonishing range of exhibits and of visitors, while the Anglia television programme on Byegones reveals a similar fascination with things from the past. It is not for nothing that 'nostalgia' has recently been pronounced a best-selling theme among books.

Various thinkers have stressed the point that family memory does not always operate in a straight continuum from generation to generation but that children often imbibe more nourishment from the past through their grandparents than their parents. In some societies this can be seen as a straight consequence of the fact that, because the mother goes out to work, 'Nanna' brings up the children. But there seems to be more to this phenomenon. Many have remarked on the natural affinity between the very young and the very old. Marc Bloch saw it in terms of the desire to skip back beyond parents, the immediate and perhaps threatening agents of change, to something more solid and immovable:

> A society that could be completely moulded by its immediately preceding period would have to have a structure so malleable as to be virtually invertebrate. It would also have to be a society in which communication between generations was conducted, so to speak, in Indian file – the children having contact with their ancestors only through the mediation of parents.
>
> Now, this is not true. . . . With the moulding of each new mind, there is a backward step, joining the most malleable to the most inflexible mentality, while skipping that generation which is the sponsor of change.[1]

If this is so, it is a great loss to their nurture that too many children are removed far from any grandparents.

Too much has been thrown away in the last half-century : our past has become as disposable as paper pants. But the primary school teacher who initiates a project on family history by asking for relics of parents' or grandparents' past can still get an embarrassing amount of stuff brought in. Different 'rooms' can be arranged in corners of the classroom and this leads on to all the questions of how they lived, what their hard times were like, what fun they had, what we have got which they had not. Children's toys are a magic link. A little girl produces a worn and treasured teddy-bear: 'This was my Grampy's and then my Daddy's, and now it is mine and I shall keep it for *my* children.' 'That's four, one after another – four generations we say.' And she nods and carefully puts Teddy in a special place. Her identity in the succession of history is secure. Old children's toys, however, when they survive, are valuable, so the next stage may be museum-visiting and then making models and collecting pictures to fill the gaps in the classroom exhibition. Old magazines and newspapers can often be dredged up to provide their vivid little pictorial advertisements of the first washing machines, ladies' corsets, gas-lights, or the first installations of bath and indoor lavatory. And the contrast in prices naturally sparks off much discussion. Thus, one way and another, the material can be gathered together for a series of constructions of family life in, say, 1960, 1940, 1920, 1900, 1880. If

[1] Bloch, *op. cit.*, p. 40.

they can be found, children's books of the period bring great joy, and scenes from one of the evocative books of reminiscence that we have, such as V. Hughes' *A London Child of the Seventies*, set the imagination going. For the life of children in the past has a clear appeal at the primary school age.

When it comes to talking or writing about the children's own family history, however, the situation can be delicate. Some stories behind those individual faces could not be happily revealed in public and questions must not be pressed. But where the stories come out with eagerness and pride they give splendid material to be shared, discussed and questioned about with the rest of the group. A miniature time-perspective begins to be formed, as through that teddy-bear, or maybe through a grandfather's war service: 'My Grandad went to India in a big ship in the war – that was a long time ago.' So children can begin to form a connection with father's or grandfather's time and this relating of oneself to the continuing time-process is very important. James Baldwin has stressed in a striking way the importance of family memory:

> What the elders have . . . that they can offer the young is the evidence in their own flesh of defeats endured, disasters passed, and triumphs won. This is their moral authority which, however mystical it may sound, is the only authority that endures; and it is through dealing with this authority that the young catch their first glimpse of what has been called the historical perspective.[1]

The felt need for a personal time perspective is well illustrated by an adult with a very meagre family history who was introduced to history for the first time through twentieth-century royal biography. She said: 'It's very interesting, but I wanted first to find the part telling what was happening when I was born.' She needed to establish her own history in relation to the kings and queens she admired so much. So, from where we ourselves appeared on the scene, memory must take us back to find out more about ourselves before that. Lord Hailsham called his autobiography *The Door Wherein I Went*[2] and implicit in that title is the sense of knowing that there is a world on the other side of that door which is still ours and which we want to go back into in imagination, because something is lacking in our experience without it. Some children today will grow up without realising that there is a door at all, yet personal experience is incomplete without a sense of that 'other room', crowded with people who are basically friendly because they belong to us. And, indeed, oral history, supported by

[1] I have been unable to trace the source of this quotation, but it was given to me as James Baldwin's.
[2] *The Door Wherein I Went*, London, 1975.

the tape-recorder, is now coming into its own in a big way.

Families belong to streets, housing estates, neighbourhoods, villages, towns; they may also belong to clubs, trade unions or churches. If the process of discovering who we are begins with family experience and family memory, it soon moves outwards into what can be a disturbing range of other societies. Indeed, for too many children family experience is minimal and too soon street groups become their society, giving what security they may. In contrast some of the happiest experiences belong to those children whose families provide the natural bridge into the larger world because they themselves are involved in bigger societies. A child who carries a flag with his parents in a May Day procession or helps his mother to sell sweets at the church bazaar is becoming a member through activity of something larger than himself and larger than his family. So he reaches another stage of finding himself through belonging. By and by he will discover that such societies as the Labour Party or the Church have longer memories and broader histories than his own immediate group; he can strike roots into a deeper past. Such children are experiencing history through participation in the life of historical groups. They are learning how to stand in their own shoes.

But what about the many for whom 'family' equals an isolated little unit (sometimes not even a unit) and who are tipped out into a chaotic scene of people scurrying here and there without recognisable purpose? This is not unlike the experience of arriving at a big railway terminus, descending from the railway carriage, which had become for a moment your home, and standing lost on the platform with no one to meet you – *you*, a solitary individual with no relationship to the eddying masses around you, except that of colliding billiard balls. Well, perhaps it is not quite as bad as that: you descend, perhaps, with a small peer-group. But this itself may be a lost little huddle. Hugeness and Confusion are two of the aspects of modern life most detrimental to the true nourishment of the young. Hugeness: the experience of being caught within something too big to grasp, something which seems to go on without end. Confusion: the apparent absence of any coherent pattern or meaning, together with the vanishing of familiar landmarks. To gain a foothold in this world, to get some understanding, at least, of what is happening to you, one must reduce size to a manageable scale and resolve confusion into patterns. The railway station ceases to be frightening when you have discovered the plan on which it is designed and how to get out of it. Pattern means a set of orderly and coherent relationships between parts: it is the antithesis of the cannoning billiard ball metaphor. Discovering pattern in communities obviously means connecting the pieces of the physical lay-out, but it means much more than mapping streets and shopping centres. The geography of communities must lead on to their histories. Why did this town or village begin just here and where was its original focus? How and why did it grow? Why do the streets go *this* way and take *these* curves? The pattern in which we grow up may for long have been a living, developing one, never static, and if we are to come to terms with continuing growth and change in our own life-time, we need to experience the sense of the living organism which is our inheritance from the past. Hope for what *we* may do in the future springs partly from what our forefathers did in the past.

This need is particularly felt when growing up in one of the huge conurbations which – for all their excitement – can be the nightmare of teaching. I remember feeling this strongly when I went to teach in London after a village childhood. My mind went back to an early experience: I remembered sitting on the hill-top, with the whole village spread below me, and thinking: '*Now* I know what I belong to. I can see its shape and size and the pattern of old and new.' Of course the sense of knowing what you belong to can be equally strong in a street neighbourhood in, for example, the East End of London, but it is not so easy to see, particularly where areas have been re-developed – many East Enders would however deny that it was impossible to feel you belonged in the old East End street. I asked myself: how could these Camberwell children grasp the meaning of their community? Fortunately in this country many conurbations – barring the artificially created new towns – are often literally a joining up of older, smaller towns or villages. Camberwell, Peckham, Kennington, Brixton had all been ancient communities long before London enveloped them. Thus the obvious way to try and show them their own 'shoes' was a project on how Camberwell village grew. This took shape in a primary school. There was plenty of material: some documents and histories, street names, houses with dates on them, styles of building, churches, chapels, schools, public buildings, the oldest shopping centres, even pillar-boxes with VR, ER VII or GR VI on them to show in which reign there arose a need for a post-box in that area. One unusual feature in this particular environment was the presence of a small park, two blocks of flats called Dover and Calais, with red-brick cats on their tops, and a small library built in the shape of a continental opera-house. Enquiry elicited the fact that all these had been planned and built by a French Huguenot family named Minet (diminutive for cat). It was an intriguing little bit of local history which sparked off the children's imaginations to try and re-create the life of these foreigners in their community. In a Battersea school, on the other hand, we concentrated, in a class of eight and nine-year-olds, on the succession of early peoples who had settled there, constructing a rhyme with accompanying pictures on the model of 'This is the House that Jack built.' 'This is the Island of Battersea. These are the Britons who lived in the Island of Battersea. These are the Romans who conquered the Britons . . . ' The reconstruction was, I fear, partly imaginary, but it was based on the meaning of the name and some archaeological remains.

Again, I recently met a group of children in a village primary school who, starting from the need to build a community on mutual support (for example, in home-making and food-growing), progressed to the need for order and pattern which they expressed by building their own model village. This 'Now' situation then became linked to the historical 'Then' of a village just after the Norman Conquest. As William I had ordered the Domesday Survey, so they would make a Domesday Book of their own village. As in this medieval village the community wrestled with law and order in the manor court, so they too would experience the problems of distinguishing truth from falsehood and combining mercy with justice in the affairs of their own imaginary village court. Thus the imagined historical situation illuminated their developing sense of what their local community was all about.

So far I have been thinking in terms of primary school experience but, of course, both family and local history must be pursued in more sophisticated ways at the secondary level. Some boys of my acquaintance buy up with their pocket money at auction sales old contraptions of all kinds, domestic and technological – a prize find was a very early knitting machine which now knits socks for all – and keep a keen eye open for any bits of industrial archaeology left lying around the countryside. The problem with this kind of interest is adequate space in which to exhibit your finds, whether at home or at school. Another way to study the life of fifty or a hundred years ago is to hunt up old magazines and guide books in junk shops. Local guide books, which are often undated, can set an intriguing puzzle: can you establish from internal evidence when this was published? One of the boys mentioned above spent a concentrated half-hour over a Lake District guide book and came up finally with a date he could prove. Here was a first-rate introduction to the method of historical deduction, and local material can set other puzzles to be solved partly by internal information and partly by knowledge of the locality. Much of this evidence concerns the technological revolution of the last hundred years and the social changes which have followed, and surely this is a natural focus of interest at the secondary stage.

There was a time when 'local history' was almost synonymous with the history of ancient monuments – the castle, abbey, cathedral, mansion and so on. It is a measure of the great shift of interest towards the 'lives of the people' that the focus is now as much on the ordinary as the extraordinary and the gap between the castle era and the present day evokes our curiosity. The spate of books guiding the young today in their exploration of local history is not only on the colourful themes of Your Castle or Coats of Arms, for Industrial Archaeology has with astonishing rapidity become a magic term in a title and the National Committee to Review Local History is even now examining the changing pattern of interest, activity and study in rural and urban history. Our history is everything up to yesterday; the unfolding of our early technology is exciting because through it an earlier version of ourselves is mirrored. In some ways communities which have grown up in close relationship to some clear physical feature – a river, a harbour, a cliff or surrounding hills – have a great advantage over those which seem to have sprung up for no clear reason in the middle of a great flat. The idea of town-building-men choosing, consciously or subconsciously, the site for their settlement can catch the imagination, perhaps particularly of those pupils who would like to be frontiersmen and women but live in a country where settlement is ancient and men's initial relationship to their environment almost buried too deep for recovery beneath the concrete – unless we make the deliberate effort to dig it up. There is, in fact, usually an interesting reason for the physical siting of even the flattest of towns in the flattest of country. The very new, consciously-made towns and vast new housing estates still have histories, albeit brief and within living memory, and can be envisaged as achievements (with good and bad in them) of men today. Why did the new towns become necessary; who took the initiative and did the planning; where did the families come from; what good points and what mistakes can we see? And the rebuilding of blitzed towns after the Second World War is a particularly stirring piece of history.

At the secondary stage discovering our past and re-living it in imagination passes into assessment and judgement. How did our grandparents' lives compare with ours? In what ways were their lives easier or harder, less or more satisfying than ours? Has the technological way of life which developed through the Industrial Revolution helped or hindered us? Are family and local problems the same now or quite different? What do we think of authority and discipline in the Victorian family? This turns us back towards ourselves and our community as the latest stage in this evolving history. One interesting way of coming at this process of assessment is through rubbish heaps. What people throw away tells a good deal about them. A town's medieval rubbish heap can be reconstructed in imagination (perhaps after a visit to the local museum) and then deductions drawn from it. A nineteenth-century one is even easier to do. To compare these with our actual twentieth-century one is most revealing. And then to pass to a reconstruction of our life today, as an excavator of rubbish heaps in a future age might do it, throws a strong and critical light on things we take for granted.

This is an appropriate point at which to consider the fact that as adolescence advances girls and boys may become more absorbed in themselves and take less interest in their environment. Even here, however, the meaning of history is not wholly absent: whether consciously or not, they still have to relate themselves to the time process through which they themselves are moving, to catch and hold their own individuality. A group of girls in a comprehensive school wrote willingly on 'Myself in ten years time'. It was, perhaps, reassuring as well as exciting to look forward and envisage both the continuity of personality and the possibility of new experiences. First, however, they were asked to write on 'It happened to me': the backward look, with its medley of memories, gave a chance for some kind of personal assessment in terms of change and development. But, while giving full weight and sympathy to this mood of self-absorption, we have still, I believe, to continue the process of helping them find themselves through the various relationships that the community offers – to discover that their own 'shoes' are bigger than they thought. And this takes us back to our memberships, voluntary and involuntary, in societies with a history.

Embedded in the general local community are these institutions and groups with their own history and traditions: churches and chapels, trade organisations, Co-ops, social and mutual aid clubs, youth clubs, cultural societies and sports clubs, and, finally, the schools themselves. The best introduction to this world, as I have suggested, is through family participation which gives the experience of purposeful membership and cooperative activity just when an incoherent world of unrelated people outside is beginning to impinge. The rôle of the school is to unfold the story of how these local associations began and grew, including the story of itself. This can begin in many places with medieval churches and with the history of medieval guilds, their many social as well as economic functions, and – for some localities – their fascinatingly detailed rules. This passes into the later study of religions, on the one hand, and the history of trade unions, on the other, both of which I want to consider a little later. In the meantime, there are local worthies to meet. There may or may not be in the locality mythical or medieval heroes or villains adorned with colourful exploits (such as Robin Hood), but there are certain to be more recent ones concerned with bettering the people's life: philanthropists, industrialists, workers' champions or beautifiers of the town. Their bearded faces look a bit stuffy in their portraits or photographs and their deeds were less dashing than those of the knights of old, but the concrete evidence of what they achieved is built into our society and therefore into our lives. If their story is told with warmth and sympathy, it can open up a world of ardour and effort which really catches the imagination. Sometimes the more light-hearted institutions are amusing to pursue: the music halls and theatres, local choirs or sports clubs. 'Half-a-crown to the doctor for stitching Humphrey Smith's chin after the match with Sutton Veny' (from the minutes of a village cricket club of the 1890s) is just one example of the half-told stories which old minute-books can yield, and old play-bills give a vivid picture of what aroused most laughter fifty or a hundred years ago.

And now we enter a wider circle of community. Young people in top secondary classes and in further education will soon be full members of the nation's political community and perhaps, even earlier, members of its economic community at work. Starting work is in itself an educational experience of the highest importance. This has been proclaimed in principle time and again, but we still fall down on the business of making this experience significant. On the economic side it should be the initiation into full adult participation at the moment when your capabilities and skills can be recognised as valuable to the community in terms of services or productions which are worth a living wage. This ought, ideally, to be a moment of pride, of self-realisation, but to achieve this demands proper initiation into the pattern of the work and your particular bit in it. And this pattern extends outwards into the geography and history and traditions of the business, into the trade union structure and workers' traditions, into the importance of this particular type of work to the whole community. Alas, all kinds of factors combine to make this experience for millions of young people, on the contrary, a dreary chore which has no recognisable purpose except to earn the wherewithal to escape into a world of one's own. How few reap the satisfaction of the boy-apprentice who was observed standing in front of a car showroom window with a group of his peers and announcing proudly: '*That's* the car I'm making part of.'

Some causes of adolescent frustration with the kind of work they are thrust into lie beyond educational remedies, for example, the complexity of modern industrial organisation and the repetitive processes still in many cases required, the dead-end jobs to which many young people are still being condemned and – even more serious – unemployment by which society refuses to the young precisely this experience of finding their own worth through recognition of it by the community. I think the vast growth of service jobs, as against directly productive ones, is also off-putting to the young who so often have a basic desire to *make* something. How much more directly did the adolescent in a primitive society experience the connection between his effort and the survival of his group! But difficult conditions can be ameliorated by a clear educational programme from the time when they first start work: in spite of great advances in initiation schemes of various kinds, too many boys and girls are flung once more into this experience of hugeness and confusion in which they find little to which they can relate themselves, unless they have the luck to work under a paternal overseer. We are still throwing away our most valuable resource in people by not seeing the entry of the young into work as a crucial stage in education. And we shall not do justice to them so long as we mismanage our economic affairs to the extent of denying them *real* work.

Returning from this digression, there is, however, a pre-work stage of learning to stand in our own shoes which belongs to the upper levels of schools and to colleges. Britain has a proud and fascinating, though disfigured, economic history. Its earlier stages mirror clearly the basic economic needs of an island society. We still have the same fundamental needs, though concealed behind our sophisticated organisation. Exploring the economic growth of our early communities can show us ourselves in all our starkest needs for survival. Such a study can be started by making our own lists of basic economic requirements and then investigating how these were satisfied at various stages in the development of our society from the primitive and medieval agricultural communities onwards. There can be some eye-openers: after 1975's drought fewer people, no doubt, believe that water simply comes out of taps, and boys and girls are not likely to be as naïve as the little city girl who, after watching the cow being milked, remarked: 'And we saw the empty milk-bottles from which the milk came that they pour into the cow,' but there are certainly many adults even who do not know that cows are not always in milk. Ecological concern is making us all much more aware of our relationship to the physical environment, but it is our own early economic history that brings this home most vividly in terms of basic physical needs and the means of satisfying them.

Britain, however, left her green pastures and small towns behind. Her dark Satanic mills spread and smoke enveloped men's activities, literally and metaphorically. The Industrial Revolution has left us an ambivalent inheritance, with some hideous aspects, yet it forms a striking story. William Blake and the Romantics reacted violently against it; reformers and philanthropists constituted a rising chorus against the evil miasma which it spread over workers' lives; we still look with horror on the remnants of back-to-back housing. Yet the inventive flair, the bold aspiration, the unrelenting effort of early industrial kings gives them a full stature of their own and – confronting them – stand the pioneers of trade unions, the Chartists, the reformers, often of even kinglier stature. The stories of these national figures furnish heroic stuff indeed, and their clashing values provoke our own views, for the pioneers of our industrial world are an essential part of ourselves, both in their achievements and in their errors. In many places, of course, the national theme can be closely linked with local or regional development. It is a subject full of opportunities for exploring values. Here is Josiah Wedgwood, building houses for his workers, yet breaking strikes in the interests of money-making. Here is your local industrialist endowing almshouses, yet pushing his workers into shocking back-to-backs. Here are your Free-Traders in Parliament, ruining ribbon-makers in Coventry in the interests of cheap food. Here are your Chartists debating the case between physical violence and political action, or your strike leaders sacrificing their starving families. There are so many themes to arouse heated discussion, leading to the forming of value-judgements and much taking of sides.

In plunging into this ambivalent area there are three principles which I believe should guide us as teachers. First, that in 'value discussions' the teacher's role is to 'hold the ring', elucidating difficulties, correcting misapprehensions or inaccurate information, willing to give his own personal judgement or to witness to his position, *if asked*, but refusing to make a pronouncement *ex cathedra*, that is, to state in absolute terms of authority which side is right and which wrong. Secondly, that one must emphasise that there *is* a right and wrong and that we ought, where possible, to decide which side we stand with. But thirdly, that the teacher has to underline the point that the 'other side' usually has a case, or at least needs to be understood with imagination. Only then can you fully understand the reasons *why* you think you are right. Rarely in conflicts of values is one side wholly right and the other wholly wrong.

Our inheritance from great reformers takes us on from economic to political action. In the current debate on how to teach political citizenship effectively and without undue bias, I take the view that the stirring history of people campaigning in the past is more effective in motivating the young than the generalised study of how institutions work, and that – rather paradoxically – involving them with people who did take sides, sometimes passionately, can teach them, out of honest debate, to form their own opinions soberly. So let us use the study of political reformers and leaders of the last two hundred years as one important form of political education. They collected evidence, listened to the case on both sides, wrote pamphlets, addressed public meetings and launched newspaper campaigns to change public opinion. Any of the great campaigns – for the abolition of slavery or child labour, for factory reform or the abolition of the Corn Laws, for urban sanitation or popular education – can become exciting stories of how people got things changed. What a school for politics Francis Place, Robert Owen and Richard Cobden – to mention three at random – provide for a new generation of coming citizens! It would be a tragedy if our traditions in this country for using the techniques of political action to effect change and end injustice passed into oblivion because we lost our history. Two characteristics can be stressed: the combination of economic action with political campaigning, and the support of disinterested philanthropists for what they saw as just causes to destroy great evils. Exploring these great campaigns opens up many techniques of citizenship, from the attempt to look at the cause of reform objectively in the Royal Commission method to the white-hot campaign that forces Parliament to take notice. Some of the nineteenth-century Royal Commission material on child labour or mining conditions is ready stuff for dramatising. When a group of about thirty-five girls turned themselves into Royal commissioners and witnesses, they drew up questions, summoned and interrogated the witnesses from employers and employees, discussed the evidence and finally re-formed themselves into Parliament to enact their own legislation on child labour. One lesson in particular was brought home: that you must listen to the mill-owners as well as the victims. In contrast to this judicious treatment, we once ran a newspaper campaign against the Corn Laws using all the journalistic devices we could muster to bring our public to the boiling point. At the secondary stage, indeed, the newspaper device can be a rewarding one: it involves imaginative and argumentative writing, giving scope for feeling and sharp debate; it gives opportunity for people of mixed ability in devising items which range from leaders, speeches and reporting to advertisements, notices of amusements and pictures.

What, then, shall we do about 'national' history? The paradox of this second half of the twentieth century is that at the very time when irresistible pressures are forcing us into world citizenship, there is a counter urge towards recovering 'national' consciousness in small ethnic or regional groups. This is, in some ways, a challenge to history, an attempt to reverse the process by which inexorably smaller groups have been swallowed by larger, a declaration against size. Viewed in this way the movement is not surprising but it does create paradox for us. While popular culture sweeps the globe, nationalists cultivate traditional languages and arts with loving care. While summit conferences wrestle with world problems, Wessex and the Isle of Dogs declare UDI. So what shall we do about initiating the rising generation into political citizenship? Wherever we are – and the answer depends very much on which part of the British Isles – we surely need to base our work first on this regional sentiment, wherever it exists. It is often rooted in legend and feeds on a romantic past: Arthur's championship of the Celtic peoples, Merlin dropping Stonehenge on Salisbury Plain, St. Brendan sailing to the Blessed Isles, Alfred burning the cakes, Bruce and the spider. The apparently less romantic Midlands can claim Guy of Warwick, the Saxon Giant-Killer and, of course, Robin Hood. As I have said, at a younger age we can savour the heroic romance of these exploits and even at a more sophisticated level we do not want to destroy pride in 'our past'.

There comes however a crucial moment when the great question 'Is it true?' has to be fully and truthfully answered. Then comes the vital process of looking at the evidence, considering the context in which the story arose, trying to sift a core of likely happening from manifest fairy tale. It can be a key moment in learning a little of the answer to that great question: 'What is truth?' The answer is seldom simple and in the case of legends we can often say 'No smoke without a fire'. Some experience must have occurred which fired the group memory and gradually its legend was developed as from age to age it was handed on through the group memory. The historical circumstances of the Israelites' flight from Egypt have been elucidated by research, but the Exodus became a group experience of high memory and symbolic value, still commemorated yearly as a promise of release to captives. The real Arthur has been projected by historical research, but whatever the limitations of this figure, King Arthur remains a symbol of chivalric warrior-leadership championing the oppressed. Our various legendary histories need not be destroyed but, reinterpreted by modern scholarship, can lead towards an understanding of the function of myth and legend in nourishing group consciousness and thence to a look at modern myths and their makers.

However strong regionalism may be, there is a common core of British memory, both proud and bitter. The hard political reality was that, by stages, the British Isles came under the rule of the British Crown. What shall we do about this common political heritage? Shall we, for instance, ditch the Kings and Queens of England? As the acquisition of a useful framework I am not against learning their dates at an early age. This is a limited exercise, like learning tables, to be knocked off in the odd half-hour. I am old-fashioned enough to think that, in suitable doses, learning by heart is both useful and enjoyable and children love getting ten out of ten for learning correctly. If not dates, at least the order of monarchs is useful general knowledge in later life, so I see no reason to abandon our little rhymes:

Willie, Willie, Harry, Steve,
Harry, Dick, John, Harry three . . .

But this, of course, is not real history, and our problem at the secondary level is what we select from British political history, if anything. I think we should ask ourselves what kinds of national achievement should form part of the group memory we are trying to pass on to the rising generation. 'Ah', you say, 'here subjective value-judgements enter in'. Yes, but selection (which implies value-judgement) there must be: thin general surveys get nowhere and even in these there is still selection concealed under a spurious objectivity. Since we still enjoy in this country freedom of syllabus-making, the selection is still ours, and we must grasp this nettle of subjectivity firmly. It is our rôle as teachers to make responsible, thoughtful choices, as fair and balanced as we possibly can, rather than following unthinkingly someone else's choice in a given course or text-book. Not that these are not often extremely useful guides, but it is our own emphases that count. If we shrink from such a responsibility, fearing the accusation of political indoctrination, we might reflect on the safeguards which pluralist choice offers as against the dangers of a possible unitary syllabus put out by the DES!

Anyway, as a try-out, let me venture some choices. Leaving aside social and economic aspects which we have already considered, I select four great positive themes in our political history: how government developed; how British men and women adventured to the ends of the earth; how we have dealt with minority groups, radicals and refugees; how we have related ourselves to the continent of Europe in hostility or friendship. You may prefer others or think my emphases misleading, but let me briefly look at the content of each.

As an introduction to the theme of how we have learned to solve our governmental problems, early laws, such as substituting a wergild (money payment) for the blood-feud, the beginnings of the jury system, ways in which medieval kings tried to stop bribery and corruption among their officials, all open up areas where actual case studies of fascinating detail can be discussed in terms of how good or bad, just or unjust the arrangements were. The 'state law' of the Star Chamber and other Tudor prerogative courts rings a modern note and points up the great question of today: is the safety of the State more important than the liberty of the individual? The way the common lawyers fought back and the Parliamentary struggle of the seventeenth century follow on. In the nineteenth century one can focus on a few of the great problems fiercely debated in Parliament – electoral reform, abolition of the Corn Laws, the government of India, the Irish Question – bringing out the pros and cons of different government policies. The issue of the monarchy is bound to come up somewhere here and must surely today be treated as an open question. Whatever our personal views, this is a prime occasion for 'holding the ring' and – since strong sentiments can be involved – insisting on careful statement and honest debate. The paperback published by Penguin on the monarchy during Jubilee Year sets the right standard, with its varying appraisals and inclusion of Willie Hamilton's case against the monarchy. The second theme of adventurers to far places hardly needs to be annotated. From early sailors to the conquerors of the North and South Poles and of Everest, it includes not only all kinds of explorers, but also missionaries, often combining bold curiosity with love of their fellow men, and religious sects seeking freedom of worship. Thirdly, how a society has dealt with those who are different or dissentient, who do not fit easily into established patterns, constitutes a crucial test by which it should be judged. What has our own record been like? To follow through from the treatment of Jews and heretics in earlier centuries to the reception of Huguenots and other refugees, the attempts to suppress radical opinion, and attitudes towards present-day immigrants, reveals actions both good and bad. There is plenty to cause shame in the telling, but the wide spectrum of tolerated difference which finally emerges in our history is an inherited 'good' which needs to be valued and guarded in the present. What is 'tolerance' and how far it can go are, again, crucial questions for today, to be discussed in the light of our history. Still more fundamental (and topical, as evidenced in television debates) is the question: What is democracy? Can it be defined simply as the rule of the majority or must our definition include the right of minorities to full consideration and protection? Finally, our love–hate relationship with Europe through the ages is a fascinating story of waves of immigrants and conquerors, of provocative fighting back, of criss-crossing influences in trade, language and social manners, of the impact of great ideas like the French Revolution, leading to the climax of collaboration in the second half of the twentieth century. Such a theme can only be treated in a series of highlights, but what a story!

As I have already suggested, we must bring out the negative aspects of what happened as well as the positive achievements, the dark spots as well as the bright. Like Oliver Cromwell, we must have our history 'warts and all'. This means the whole face of history, good and bad together – not an imbalance either way. The glories of the Elizabethan Age have to be balanced by the more sinister activities of the Star Chamber and the plight of vagabonds; the evils perpetrated by the British Raj in India by their system of communications and enthusiasm for preserving the Indian heritage. For the most valuable citizens are those who can look with clear eyes at the society to which they belong. It is easy to stand outside and snipe in criticism; it is comforting to blinker yourself on the inside and believe or pretend that your nation or group is always right; it is much more difficult but much more important to cultivate in any group context the quality of critical loyalty, of making a critical scrutiny *from within* a position of involvement. The need today to involve the next generation in its country's affairs hardly needs stressing. They are not likely to fall into the error of 'my country, right or wrong', but rather into the opposite one of critical non-involvement. Thus the drive of a course in British history has to be towards generating the attachment of critical citizens. Ultimately Parliamentary democracy depends precisely, not on 'my party, right or wrong', but on open-eyed and responsible judgement as to where, in a perpetually ambivalent situation, you should throw the weight of your commitment. It is a question of standing squarely in our own shoes – even when we know where they pinch.

So we reach the outermost circle of world citizenship. This is a concept which has been pushed in the last decades by many reformers of the curriculum and the logic behind the advocacy of courses in world history is undisputable. The whole world is indeed tied in one bundle, but, as a rule, we must work from the smaller to the larger, the inner to the outer. It is true that far distant parts of the world can come zooming into children's consciousness at a very early age through various bits of personal experience (a father sent out to Kuwait, a brother in the police force of Hong Kong, or a Japanese radio) and we can certainly make capital out of these. But more formally structured courses in world history surely belong quite late in the secondary stage. It is the largeness of scale and therefore the tendency to large generalised statements that causes the difficulty. In the early days of such courses text-books were often dull and off-putting because there was no space in which to paint a detailed picture and the broad washes seemed almost necessarily drab. Techniques in writing have much improved, but the problem will always be that of combining largeness and minuteness together. In many ways the values implicit in teaching world history belong to my next chapter on the experience of 'difference'. The point to be made here is that fostering local or national loyalties is not in real conflict with developing a sense of the oneness of all peoples.

But there are great international communities which inspire powerful feelings of membership yet have been – still are – divisive in their impact: I mean the great religions of the world. For many British children their family religious commitment, if they have one, still lies in one of the Christian denominations, but today we have the other main world religions in our midst as never before. Here is a form of 'belonging' which has played a crucial role in the formation of cultures and still does. In the British Isles this heritage from the past is chiefly, though not exclusively, Christian. To neglect it would be untrue to our history. The experiences of saints, martyrs and missionaries, the lives of monks and the sufferings of the persecuted, the anonymous toil of medieval church builders and the fire of later evangelical preachers, these and many other memorable treasures of history belong to our inheritance. From the story of local churches and chapels to the religious symbolism embodied in great national ceremonies, such as the Coronation Service, from the great Christian charities of the past to the many agencies of Christian compassion today, our society is shot through with Christian feeling and activity. Even the conventions that still shape the pattern of our lives – the working week, the 'Sabbath rest', the holidays at Christmas and Easter go back to Judeo-Christian origins, while the band's rendering of 'Abide with me' at football matches is a remarkable survival. All this needs to be opened up for the next generation. Yet in a multi-racial society there are those other great religious heritages to acknowledge. Can we hold the hard position of giving positive sympathy and appreciation to all the varying religious traditions which may be represented in our school groups, while recognising that specific loyalty to one of them calls us to real commitment without bigotry? In some contexts the problem is not so much clashing religious inheritances as the non-commitment of indifference or hostility. Either way, a common factor remains: Man's search for God has been a crucial and universal element in his history, that is, in the making of ourselves, hence the religious dimension in community history can only be ignored by those really blinded by prejudice. Indeed, recent television programmes suggest that there is a felt need to explore this heritage.

It will by now be obvious that, in trying to write about the historical experience of learning to stand in our own shoes, I have involved myself in very awkward questions of values. These cannot be evaded. As soon as we begin to talk in terms of 'the historical experience' instead of 'learning history', we have placed the subject in a dimension where such questions continually call for consideration and judgement. The rôle of the teacher becomes dangerous, but exciting and worthwhile. 'I refuse to become involved', one said. 'Then', I submit, 'You are not a teacher of history'. 'But', said another, 'You cannot come out of the study of history without becoming a more compassionate human being.'

3
Standing in other people's shoes

It is strange that human beings thrive on both 'likeness' and 'difference' – mixed in the right proportions. Children's need for this mixture is somewhat analogous to their need for both 'soft' and 'hard' experiences, that is, situations in which they can do as they like and situations in which their freedom is disciplined and limited by coming up against the demands of others. The analogy lies in the fact that it is easier to relate yourself to people in your own environment than to surmount the barriers which are obstacles to understanding the different. Of course likeness and difference intermingle (in certain senses there is plenty of both in family life) but, broadly speaking, we relate ourselves in one way within the groups to which we belong and in another way to people from evidently different backgrounds. The two experiences have a different quality, even though they can intermingle. Just as there may still be educational theorists of the school of thought which believes that hard experiences stunt the growth of personality, so there may be those who argue that any historical topic which at first sight appears off-putting, not easily grasped as immediately relevant, is a useless and meaningless piece of junk. Teachers with a sociological approach admit within their schemes the history which explains the immediate social environment, but what possible relevance, some argue, can there be in shipping the class off to ancient Athens or the Crusades? Instant relevance demands quick returns.

The operative word in this discussion is 'relationship'. A piece of remote history can indeed be taught in such a way as to be quite meaningless because no attempt is made to establish any relatedness, but the same topic can be wonderfully enriching when a relationship is created which opens up a new world. The historical experience of difference adds a new dimension to the notion of relevance. By 'difference' here I mean the experience of encountering other people (whether as individuals or groups) whose first impact upon us is one of 'otherness', whether in their appearance, language, way of life, or modes of thought and feeling. This encounter can, of course, take place through geographical studies as well as historical. The former is simpler to defend in terms of immediate relevance: some circumstance may easily take the young or their fathers to the ends of the earth, so that the people of Singapore or the Pacific become quickly related to them. The understanding of people remote in time often needs more effort than that of people remote in place but there are cogent reasons for claiming that to live in imagination in certain periods of history can be both enjoyable and stimulating. First, without implying any full recapitulation theory, it is obvious that primary school children get great satisfaction out of playing at primitive man, just as they do in pretending to be Red Indians or cowboys. We can enlarge their pleasure by giving them, in suitable form, genuine archaeological and historical materials to enrich their play. Allied to this is the treasure-trove instinct which inspires children to dig and makes the work of an archaeologist something which will excite their curiosity and fire them to participate. Secondly, although modern civilisation supplies many vicarious adventures and exploits on television (both fictitious and real), this is no reason why boys and girls should be cut off from the wealth of stories which explorers and adventurers of all ages in history have left us. Indeed, the mass media have responded well here. Television is ready to transport us into stirring and exciting adventures of history which have the great advantage that the people are real. Thirdly, for many boys and girls life is pretty limited in scope and variety, materially comfortable perhaps, but drab and starved of colour and beauty. Their imaginations need to be fed on strange new worlds, rich in colour and shape, opening up to them delightful escape and further possibilities. Fourthly, the experience of historical difference can startle and stimulate into excitement, giving a new look to our own age. Perhaps others would formulate their reasons differently, but we should all agree that, in this aspect, history is for pleasure – the pleasure that enriches.

My four points can take a little comment. First, the primitive play motif. It can justifiably be argued that this activity is not one of 'doing history' at all but simply imaginative play. I recall a group of seven-year-olds who, once launched into the life of early hunters, brought their own woolly animals to school, hunted them with verve round the room, cooked and ate them with imaginary relish and were prepared to repeat this process *ad infinitum*. But play can be linked with evidence in the shape of artefacts and gradually this group was brought to a realisation that we were playing at real people who had left us stone axes and cooking pots. Rôle play in a world where operations were simpler and work more directly linked to results can be extended from primitive life to, for instance, the medieval village, where historical evidence is much fuller. We can live in the shoes of the ploughman or the cowherd who play real parts, of satisfying importance, in the life of their village. This gives imaginative compensation for the hugeness and complexity in which so many children's lives are caught, and if the oxherd has straw in his hair because he has to sleep with his oxen, so much the better. Detectives have high prestige among children and so their treasure-trove instinct can be developed into the game of playing detective in looking for all kinds of clues that lead us to the people of the past. Their environment today naturally sharpens most children's powers of observation concerning everything mechanical around them, but curiosity about the evidences of the past which also lie around them needs fostering.

The explorer motif is a perpetual theme with the young. It might seem that space exploration, with its astounding achievement in technical training and equipment, had wholly taken over this area of interest, but is there not a difference – almost a counter-appeal – in the one-man show and the small group who set out with the barest, simplest equipment? To become a Space Man may be the long-term ambition of many a child who knows very well that this is hard to attain and almost beyond his reach. In the meantime to stand in the shoes of a Viking chief setting out across the Atlantic or of Marco Polo crossing the Gobi desert gives an immediate experience in which boldness to challenge as yet unconquered forces of nature and ingenuity to meet emergencies count for more than sophisticated knowledge or apparatus. And even in the twentieth century we still respond with a thrill to the histories of men and women pitting their bare individual power against the stark elements in conquering Everest or reaching the South Pole, or sailing the ocean in tiny boats. The heroic material of history right through the ages is a vast treasure house for our delight and inspiration.

The desire to escape into fantastic worlds of the imagination is a deep human urge. We see it in a tragically pathetic form in the dream interlude of *West Side Story*. Fiction, films and plays offer one kind of escape; history offers another. Here is a world, not of unreality, but of reality outside our own experience. It is strange but true. It opens windows on unimagined beauties and terrors and sets the imagination free in these new realms. I am not suggesting, however, that all these experiences are on a lofty plane. It was the gorgeous palace of the Kublai Khan, with its red and green dragons, that excited one group of boys and the fabulous wardrobe of Queen Elizabeth I that captured some girls. Primary school children don their knight's armour in a twinkling and flourish the brilliant sign-language of heraldry in the face of foe or friend. Rich visual imagery even if it has to be enjoyed with the eyes of the imagination alone is an important element in the historical experience.

Sometimes the whole setting of an historical topic gives an experience that compensates for present dreariness or limitation. A group of girls who wrote a play about St. Francis certainly responded to this strange and beautiful character, but it was the Italian scene that most caught their imaginations. Living in an undeniably ugly part of London, they fastened on the picture of sunshine and flowers which the story evoked. In their play their chief prop became an almond tree in flower, manufactured from a dead tree branch with bits of pink crepe paper stuck all over it. That almond tree became a symbol of something they were missing in their environment. They asked to keep it, and one wretched November evening, while the fog and fish-and-chip smells rolled around, they set it up at the end of their street and acted their play for their Mums and Dads. Escape? Yes, certainly. But, you may say, doesn't escape have a morally debilitating effect? I think we can distinguish between bad and good escape. Bad escape is into a fantasy world of such absorbing unreality that it unfits the dreamer to return to his real, limited world. Good escape I should describe as living for a spell in a world which is real but 'other' than our own, which refreshes and exhilarates without binding us under a spell which we cannot break. Its test is that we return to our own lives with more, not less, power to cope. Those girls playing St. Francis brought their Italian experience of history right back with them into their back street. It is, of course, important to remember that 'real' must be extended to cover another category of archetypal symbolism, as in such fairy-tales as Beauty and the Beast, but our concern here is with history as reality.

Finally, there is the experience of coming up against people and their ideas of such a qualitative difference that, in startling, they sometimes repel, so that the initial relationship can be one of hostility, not delight. A present-day student, asked to prepare an outline of Dante's argument for universal monarchy, arrived in class in a state of indignation: 'I can't do it' she said 'his ideas repel me too much'. It was fascinating to watch how, as class discussion proceeded, she submitted herself to the process of trying to understand someone she had thought she disagreed with so profoundly. She ended by urging us forward through the Divine Comedy: 'I've got to get to Paradise', she said. The group finally agreed that it was not only fair to ask them to study people with alien ideas, but positively rewarding, both in the process of trying to get inside those puzzling personalities and in the new human understanding that resulted. These were college students; one would not expect such a sophisticated awareness of what was happening to them from most secondary school students, but their educational experience can be similar: the challenge of new viewpoints which disturb our preconceived notions, the attempt to understand with sympathy before condemning and shutting out, the new dimension which opens up when the imagination has taken into its scope strange, undreamt-of characters.

Thus history as the experience of standing in other people's shoes instead of our own is relevant in the sense that it provides experiences which, because they are, or can become, enjoyable, are taken into the imagination and enrich the whole personality. There are also lessons to be learnt which we will consider a little later, but my main contention is that the young can *enjoy* historical worlds other than their own and that we deny this nourishment to their imaginations at our peril. To play at King Arthur, or sail strange seas, or revel in the riches of Akbar's court, or puzzle over the asceticism of medieval monks are all forms of living experience which we, as history teachers, have in our gift.

But can we, or do we, give gifts such as these? How do we get the young launched into these strange worlds when so often their initial inclination, not to say prejudice, is against anything 'old'? The argument for environmental studies and for the history of ourselves is that you can start with things present in immediate experience, so that the young can begin at once to explore for themselves. This is in keeping with modern methodology to which the old 'teacher's talk' is anathema. But to transport to strange worlds needs a magic carpet. Clearly the most obvious magic carpet available is supplied almost free of charge in television and radio programmes, in films and in audio-visual tapes. How fortunate we are: switch on, and all the magic in the world can be had almost at the drop of a hat! With such colourful expertise to command, why should the ordinary teacher try to be a story-teller any more? In spite of the very great riches given us by the mass media, I have a certain sneaking regret about the abdication of the teacher, for two reasons. First, it is all too easy and therefore liable to be undervalued by watchers or listeners who grow blasé about the feast offered. Secondly, story-telling is an ancient and universal human art, a method *par excellence* by which the older generation has always passed on its wisdom, so why should we let the experts monopolise it? Of course, as school teachers, we cannot command the rich resources of sight and sound which the mass media have, but there is an immediacy about an exciting story told directly, person to person, which cannot be matched by what appears in the box or over the air. So I hope the teacher who can communicate through words will not forego his or her ancient role as *speaker*. In primary schools it is still crucial, I believe, that teachers should be story-tellers. At the secondary stage an oral introduction has, of course, to be more sophisticated, but still the essence of it is a vivid, intriguing bit of narrative that whets the curiosity. To transport the group to strange worlds the spoken word must be *with power*. It is itself the magic carpet; no one is going to move an inch above the classroom floor unless the 'lifting power' of words and gestures is present. Once transported to the new realm, however, exploration and discovery must be theirs. If we liken the study of history to the investigation of a new territory, there are three ways of doing it. You can fly over the top in a general survey: this is the undiluted teacher's lesson. You can enter it on the ground and follow a well-blazed trail: this is teacher-directed study. You can enter with your leader who then says: 'Now scatter and explore!' This is the combination of oral stimulus and individual research. Sometimes, I concede, the initial stimulus does not come from the teacher's initiative but, after all, from a television programme, or some exotic find, even something read in the newspaper, but, on the other hand, I have met a class where a television 'carpet' that could have got moving fell flat for lack of a little vivid motive-force from the teacher. The magic carpet works in various ways, but locomotive force from here to there is the essential requirement.

But when arrived, how much can we really enter into other people's experience? This is a question often debated by historians. Are we so conditioned by our own circumstances as to be totally unable to encounter the 'other' with any real degree of open-ness? Some would argue so, and most would agree that our own framework of reference must necessarily condition to some extent our approach to the new and strange. Each generation must feel, and so re-write, the history of the past in its own terms: in this sense, as Croce said, all history is contemporary history. But to deny the total possibility of meeting the unfamiliar with some degree of open-ness is a view of despair. How otherwise do we enlarge our understanding of human-beings in their infinite variety except by developing a willingness to encounter what is really there and let it make its own impact on us? This is the essence of real encounter, whether it be with the living contemporary or the historical dead. It is one of the most highly educative experiences and therefore we must surely try to create the conditions in which the next generation can enter into it. But the problem goes deeper. Granted the willingness to be open in encounter, how possible is it to get inside a really alien past? The thinking of R.G.Collingwood is useful to us here. The historian, he thought, was concerned with the 'inside' as well as the 'outside' of an event:

> By the outside of the event I mean everything belonging to it which can be described in terms of bodies and their movements: the passage of Caesar . . . across a river called the Rubicon at one date, or the spilling of his blood on the floor of the senate-house at another. By the inside of the event I mean that in it which can only be described in terms of thought: Caesar's

defiance of Republican law, or the clash of constitutional policy between himself and his assassins.[1]

He goes on to argue that getting inside the event means for the historian re-thinking the thoughts that shaped it: 'all history is the re-enactment of past thought in the historian's own mind'.[2] More recently, Vivian Galbraith wrote: 'Events will not of themselves teach us much until we can speak the thoughts of the men responsible for them.'[3] Collingwood and Galbraith probably both over-emphasised the purely intellectual thought-element, but the idea of the inside of an event lights up what we are trying to do. At a simpler level, no doubt, than that of the professional historian, the activity of exploring historical experience in school means seeking to re-enact in mind and imagination, not only the thoughts but the feelings of these people of the past. Re-enactment could not possibly be exactly the same as the original happening. Limitations are there. Thoughts, and to some extent, feelings, can be recorded and therefore can be re-thought or felt, but physical sensation – the pain of wounds, the exhaustion of long horse-back riding, the smell and taste of those grapes which the first explorers to Virginia found so delightful – these can only be imagined as we think we might have experienced them, whilst the human emotions of history run well beyond our range at both ends, both in exaltation and in terror. Moreover, Collingwood suggests that it is difficult to get inside a *completely* alien world, and, of course, there are the limitations of actual personal experience among the young for whom we are planning. In spite of all these reservations, the attempt is worth while, but in choosing our topics of 'difference' it is crucial that in the new and the strange there should be links of common experience to latch on to. Ultimately, the claim that we can in some degree enter through sympathetic imagination into experiences of difference rests, paradoxically enough, on the *common* elements of human nature which bind men of all ages and all races together.

I want now to consider for a moment two of the most extraordinary people in history to examine the rewards which come from exploring their experience: Socrates and Dante. To students in top groups of secondary schools or sixth-form colleges they can, as I have already suggested in the case of Dante, be both attracting and repelling, and it is this combination which is so stimulating. Take some of the main elements in the story of Socrates, as interpreted by Plato: his

[1] R. G. Collingwood, *The Idea of History*, Clarendon Press, 1946, Oxford Paperbacks, 1961, p. 213.
[2] *op. cit.*, p. 215.
[3] V. Galbraith, *Domesday Book: Its Place in Administrative History*, Clarendon Press, 1974, p. 170.

background in that maddening democracy of Athens, so active, so quarrelsome, and based on slave labour; his role as a disturbing teacher, making the young question traditional assumptions and think for themselves; the accusations made by an insecure government, worried because they see his disruptive influence as an attack on the majority; Socrates' defence of himself as a good citizen; the reasons for his condemnation, and Socrates' refusal to evade death because, as a good citizen, he must bow to the city's sentence; his discussions with his friends and disciples on the immortality of the soul; his manner of dying. How remote from the present-day world and yet how many bells that noble story persistently rings for us in the late twentieth century! It leads into discussions of the nature of democracy and whether it demands majority suppression of minority views, freedom of thought versus the safety of the State, when the good citizen should protest and when obey, the way people face death and the possibility of a future life. Although the actual language of Plato's dialogues may be too difficult, some of the arguments used are well within the reach of the young people we have in mind. Through it all runs the encounter with a great but perhaps irritating individualist – the gadfly of society as he called himself. And it is appropriate to end by asking: Should *we* have liked him? What would *we* have done with him? If the comparison does not offend, a somewhat similar treatment of the life of Jesus suggests itself as giving, at the very least, such a searching encounter.

I once had the experience of lecturing on Dante to a group of sixth-form college students on a Friday evening. It was a most unpropitious time and I was uncertain as to whether the surprisingly large audience was due to staff pressure or the attraction of the subject – but I doubted the latter. However that may have been, by the end of the evening I had realised, through the questions and discussion that ensued, the rich possibilities of Dante's life and vision for a general audience of older teen-agers. Initially he can certainly repel. 'Did he not believe in hell and enjoy putting his enemies there? How arrogant he was!' Think again! Here was a man who loved passionately and lost his love, went into Florentine politics, lost again and was exiled for life, put his faith for the salvation of his chaotic world in one world emperor (the 'dictator', if you like) and saw his faith collapse again politically, wandered for years, eating 'the bitter bread of exile' and, with all his great talents, was shut out of any satisfying participation in human affairs. Half his life was that of a frustrated refugee, and yet his crowning work was a vision of the unity and purpose of all human living under the judgement, which is the love, of the ruler of the universe. Whether we agree with it or not, this was undoubtedly a magnificent affirmation of meaning in human living, establishing what we have known again in this century, that the human spirit can rise above persecution, exile and frustration in creative response. Even a student from so different a culture as the Chinese responded to this encounter in an essay which he entitled: 'Dante, a loser in love and politics, but a winner in his world vision'. Matter for discussion is as varied as Dante's own life. Does Dante's love-affair with Beatrice resemble in any sense a modern boy–girl experience? How could a dead Beatrice become his inspiration? Does Dante's argument for world government make sense today? The Divine Comedy is really about life in this world, although located in the next, and Dante's ideas about sin and punishment, for instance, can rouse furious thought and discussion. Why did he think people who break relationships, sow discord and disrupt society were so much worse than illicit lovers like Paolo and Fransesca? Why are suicides in hell? Why is Dante so concerned about free will? What kind of 'happiness' do the people in paradise have? Dante's framework of vision was so different from ours, and yet we see clearly how, because the basic elements in human experience remain so much the same, some, at least, of his visionary encounters come home to us with great force. Admittedly he speaks in a difficult language which has to be not only translated but interpreted: here the obstacles of 'difference' are a challenge and our rôle as teachers is to convince that effort to get behind them is worth while.

I have deliberately chosen two rather remote examples which you may well think to be too esoteric because the right kind of material about them is not so easy to lay hands on. This is true, but there are, of course, many other more accessible characters whose lives and thoughts are gold-mines for the kind of exploration I have tried to outline. The essential ingredients are that they should be people who belonged to, but challenged their own age, who lived courageously and sought strenuously for answers to the human predicaments they encountered, who had some kind of vision and could communicate it in words of power. Since success in 'putting them over' depends partly on enthusiasm about them, all teachers who feel able should make their own selection. My purpose in being rather pig-headedly ancient and medieval in my personal choice was to demonstrate a conviction that, provided we can find the right kind of language in which to interpret them, there are so many more grand men and women waiting off-stage to be introduced to the rising generation than just the old gang who have appeared so often (and sometimes so wearisomely).

The notion of having to make an effort to break down barriers of communication has a sniff of the 'hard' rather than the 'soft' in education. I would reiterate that history is for enjoyment – that pleasure which sweeps you clean out of yourself in delight with that which is not yourself – but the exhilaration of such experiences should send us back to ourselves and our own world with two quite hard lessons learned. In the first place, we should have learned not to throw up instant defences against strange and disturbing ideas which cause discomfort, insecurity, even fear. An instinct for self-preservation so often tempts us to buttress ourselves in our own opinions against anything that might threaten them. We approach the alien with suspicion, judge it too rapidly, label it with a label of hostility – Marxist, Fascist, religious fanatic, atheist, bourgeois, racist or whatever – and thereafter speak to nothing but the label. This 'labelling habit' is the enemy of all true dialogue, all encounter with difference, and, alas, even as teen-agers we may already be developing it. It is, perhaps, the most divisive factor in our society today. Everyone, of course, has an ideology of sorts, in the simple sense of a framework of values and beliefs into which new ideas are received, but what I would call a fortress ideology, i.e. a rigid system which maintains its strength by claiming that it contains the whole truth and nothing but the truth, forms an intractable and dangerous element in present-day communities. The beginning of wisdom is to understand that one group rarely possesses the whole truth and that no 'enemy' is without a grain of truth. The 'sowers of discord' who shout their hostile labels at each other and refuse to communicate with any except the like-minded can create a hell in modern society, as they did in Dante's day.

The historical experience will certainly not cure us of this evil in a trice, but the practice of exploring alien, perhaps unpalatable points of view with careful sympathy and imagination, of seeking to understand before judging, of opening oneself with courage to what may disturb, can certainly help towards forming a habit of positive tolerance. By this I mean, not indifference, not a sloppy blurring of real differences, but respect for difference, where possible, and, at the very least, endeavour to understand what one is driven to oppose utterly. Moreover, history shows, amongst other things, how little of completely black or white there is in the doings of men. Evil, in persons or in groups, can be good gone wrong, the potentially great good sometimes being corrupted into great evil. We recoil from the burnings of the Inquisition, yet the high-minded dedication to the saving of souls which possessed many Inquisitors tells us another truth, and there are as many ambivalent situations in history as in contemporary life. The holy man in the Egyptian desert who was a fourth-century 'drop-out'; Edward III's knights of the Garter who were capable of butchering the inhabitants of a town by the noble laws of chivalry; John Newton writing hymns with a cargo of African slaves below deck – such happenings cause us puzzlement but are well worth wrestling with to understand. Cultivating the open mind emphatically does not mean abandoning convictions of our own, but rather seeking a fruitful encounter while remaining sturdily ourselves. If we think of our own framework of ideas as the house we inhabit, encounter means, not breaking down the house, but enlarging it to give house-room to strangers. There was once a splendid joke in the *New Statesman,* culled from a notice in a church magazine, which thanked the anonymous donor of couplers to the organ 'which enabled the organist to change his combinations without moving his feet'. Real encounter can be rather like that.

In the second place, if history can shake us out of a too like-minded huddle, it can also bring us back from other worlds to see our own and ourselves in a new light. We can, indeed, really only measure our own living by contrast and comparison with other ages and civilisations. Without this yard-stick we sink into an unseeing, unaware kind of existence. From the pre-industrial ages, for instance, we can come back with heightened perceptions to assess the pros and cons of our comfortable standard of living, our use of the natural world, our technological triumphs, our mass habitation sites. Take a succession of scenes through the ages – an Athenian gymnasium, a medieval cloister or school, a Renaissance group of music-makers, an Elizabethan play at the Globe, an eighteenth-century street scene, an unreformed Parliamentary election – how sharp the contrasts when juxtaposed to contemporary scenes of today and how eye-opening the discussion which can follow! It is hard to attain Burns' 'to see ourselves as others see us', but in historical exploration we can return from the experience of trying to stand in other people's shoes to a new awareness of the size and fit of our own shoes.

4
Generating power to live

Power to live a properly human life is generated, in part at least, out of memory. Without memory, as I have said, we should be two-dimensional people – a state difficult to imagine. We respond or act in the present and prepare for the future in the light of our experience heretofore and the values we have formed through it. Life, it is true, has to be lived forwards, but it can only be understood backwards. If our memory resources are limited to our own brief lives, our responses in living are likely to be weak and trivial, for, says a recent writer, 'we cannot base our decisions only on our experiences of the present. That would be like a swimmer trying to hold on to the waves.'[1] Another recent writer sees the significance of memory thus:

> It is the glory of man alone to use and develop his power of memory and by that means to find continuity, integrity and purpose in his life. [2]

Memory is history and it was Collingwood who made the classical statement about the purpose of history which linked it firmly to the question of present living:

> What is history for? ... My answer is that history is 'for' human self-knowledge. It is generally thought to be of importance to man that he should know himself, where knowing himself means knowing not only his mere personal peculiarities, the things that distinguish him from other men, but his nature as man. Knowing yourself means knowing, first, what it is to be a man; secondly, knowing what it is to be the kind of man you are; and thirdly, knowing what it is to be the man you are and nobody else is. Knowing yourself means knowing what you can do; and since nobody knows what he can do until he tries, the only clue to what man can do is what man has done. The value of history, then, is that it teaches us what man has done and thus what man is.[3]

---

[1] Jürgen Moltmann, *The Center Magazine*, Nov./Dec., 1977.
[2] B. Nolan, *The Gothic Visionary Perspective*, Princeton University Press, 1977, p. 87.
[3] Collingwood, *op. cit.*, p. 10.

In the last two chapters we have been reflecting on two types of historical knowledge which give us a longer perspective on ourselves and a wider understanding of humanity, doing, in fact, just what Collingwood says. Behind these types of experience lies the fundamental *raison d'être* for history (indeed, for the 'humanities' as a whole) that the store-house of past human experience, in giving self-knowledge, generates power for present living.

I want in this chapter to explore a little more deeply what history tells us about the springs of human vitality, as this finds expression in response, choice and action. At once, we come on the paradox that personal freedom at its highest expresses itself in commitment. It is the uncommitted person, the drifter blown about by every passing whim, who is the unfree one. History, it is true, shows the dangers of uncritical or fanatical commitment which we have already touched upon, while it also shows that inheriting a historical commitment can sometimes indeed be a form of imprisonment from which people are constrained to break loose. Yet the kind of vitality which characterises a pioneer society that has cut its cables with the past also takes its toll. Jürgen Moltmann commenting on the American experience, says: 'While the footlooseness of Americans as pioneers was a source of vitality and charm, several of the new forms that the accelerating rootlessness of Americans is taking should be cause for alarm.'[1] I have already argued that, in the main, to be born into a situation of historic membership gives the necessary security for good growth, but – pressing the point further – I would claim that it nourishes the ability to live with power. By power here I do not mean political or economic power (although these may become part of it) but simply power to make a significant impact on one's situation, however narrow or extended that may be. This historical membership, as we have already noted, may be in a religious organisation, a trade union or political party, or some other society, even a cultural club. The point is that it introduces the young to a society with a cause, in which present members take a pride in past achievements and, as it were, wire their own activities to this power house of the past. Of course some of the next generation react by pointedly 'doing their own thing' in disassociation from the tradition. On the other hand, traditional commitments can lead to a perpetuation of divisiveness in which historical memory is tragically powerful. Nonetheless, purpose in future activity is partly at least generated out of the history of past commitments.

In the last two hundred years or so, the two most widely felt commitments in this country have probably been to religious groups

[1] Moltmann, *loc. cit.*

or to the new struggling workers' movements. Now, the first has declined in influence and the second has greatly changed its character, but both still embody powerful loyalties and deep historical memories. The noble army of martyrs and leaders in the struggle to win human rights for ordinary people can still bring a thrill in the telling of their story. Whatever view we take of religious commitment, history shows us an astonishing range of people who have been propelled into all kinds of action by this force. Now it is obvious that the actual workings of such commitments do not, as a rule, belong to the sphere of public education, but rather to the very important educational rôles of family and social organisms. But as power inherent in the record of the past, such themes are very much grist to our mill. If in school we are to nourish the spiritual energies and resources of the rising generation, we must not suppress the power of these great forces as they come at us out of the pages of history. The stuff we handle as teachers of history has dynamite in it and we have a choice between trying to defuse it, that is, belittling human endeavour by cynical comment or letting forth the full power of enthusiasm and passionate commitment. In my belief we sneer at enthusiasm to our peril. Indeed, I would like to see the topic of 'enthusiasm' as one of the historical studies at the top of the school. Think what a variety of examples one could chose – from St. Paul to Martin Luther King, Mahomet or Francis Xavier to the Chartists and the Suffragettes. We may disagree with their commitments, but if history, in one of its facets, is to show the drive of great purposes and heroic struggles we must not cut them down to petty proportions.

In the present political climate the hardest type of emotion to handle with sincerity is that of national loyalty. In a world more and more drawn together, we recoil from the divisiveness of extreme patriotism, just as we have repudiated an arrogant jingoism, or the claim to be fighting a wholly 'just war'. On the other hand, we see the country falling apart into regionalism and stricken with racial division. Can a multi-regional and multi-racial society achieve any solidarity of purpose, and is there enough common heritage of history to feed fuel to this national loyalty? We do not know today. We know it could be done in 1940. One of the noticeable features at that moment was the way in which, in the mass media, in speeches and so on, the memory of the Armada victory was resurrected. History was used to fuel national resolution. We should not all agree with Winston Churchill's interpretation of British history, but there can be no doubt that his sense of history enhanced his awareness of the momentous crisis facing Britain in 1940 and spurred him to rise to its challenge. Moreover, the heroics of those speeches he made to rouse his countrymen drew part of their strength from the conviction that we could not repudiate our past. It was because he articulated what many were feeling that the magic worked. Occupied countries, too, could draw comfort from their history. After the war I was told by a curator in the Oslo museum that, when exasperated by a high German official who was belittling the magnificent Viking boats there, he had replied: 'There is one interesting thing about those boats: we really did successfully invade England in them.'

In contrast, those who have felt impelled to stand outside the national effort in obedience to a different commitment, can also carry inspiration for today. I recently heard of a secondary school student who made Conscientious Objectors her special study. She drew up her own list of questions and then visited and taped conversations with as many objectors as she could track down from World War II, even, I believe, running to earth one or two surviving voices from the First World War. She wanted to discover for herself why people made such a stand and what it felt like to be outside the mass enthusiasm. So here was a young person from the rising generation deliberately choosing to relate herself to a piece of historical experience which may well have appeared puzzling, but also courageous and strangely noble.

Other battles against enemies of the spirit have to be fought now. In political terms we have to discover new meanings to words such as liberty, equality, democracy, political responsibility. The memory of old battles must not be allowed to become imprisoning, yet the haunting question for us is whether the inhabitants of this island today can still find inspiration in 'our past' to stiffen their wills in present need – and what do we here mean by 'our'? At the moment I really do mean British history (in large measure, though not exclusively) and here is the rub. For some this is the natural inheritance: the values for which Roundheads and Cavaliers fought, the issues on which the belligerent John Wilkes challenged the establishment, the tactics used to force through the 1832 Parliamentary Reform are not only material for critical discussion but a source of political inspiration. The first school success I recall was for an impassioned imaginary speech purporting to be made by Cromwell in the Long Parliament. Years later I discovered that there was a case for the Royalists, but my first 'political effort' did inculcate a belief in politics as a matter of high principle, rather than a 'dirty game'. Again, the debate on the Corn Laws and Free Trade, with their clashing of sectional interests, and the final resolution of the conflict, with the spectacle of a politician ruining his political career because convinced by the Opposition arguments, struck home to me as an inspiring example of democratic politics in action. No doubt this was all very naïve, and today we see that we must weave in those darker themes of minorities repressed and the unfree oppressed. Moreover, the past on which the rising generation in Britain draws is much more deeply mixed. As children, my generation could legitimately think of 'our heritage' as the development of British political democracy, but today it is unthinkable not to incorporate with it those immigrant inheritances that have come to stay and are a further source of our enrichment. The moral fibre of Muslim society, the cohesion of African and Indian families are examples of social inheritances which we must recognise and value. If heritage is to be a cohesive and not a divisive force, generating power for constructive action today, these other traditions have to be married with British democratic values.

The inspiration to be drawn from great human spirits is obviously not confined to 'our own'. I have already spoken about the enjoyment of standing in other people's shoes, and I would now carry the point further, for great men of all times and nations can be a source of power today. A small boy, introduced for the first time to a historical hero, exclaims with shining eyes: '*I* might be great one day!' A new dimension in the possibilities of living is opening up for him. When I was about ten I received as a birthday present a large and rather solemn volume of Lives which told me on the title-page:

> Lives of great men all remind us
> We can make our lives sublime,
> And departing leave behind us
> Footprints in the sands of time.[1]

Those footprints fascinated me, for I could not see how you made them. We need quite a different metaphor for the subtle process of responding to human grandeur: there seems to be a kind of osmosis operating through the imagination by which our whole sense of human potentiality is enlarged. This kind of response has been described as 'passionate sympathetic involvement' in which there is 'an inter-penetration' of realities.

If you just let a procession of your own favourites pass before your eye of vision you will realise how your sense of human meaning would be impoverished if they did not inhabit your memory in such a way as to be evoked at will. Of Socrates, Dante and Cromwell I have already spoken, but consider Pericles rousing the Athenians, Alexander reaching out to the Indus, Augustine proclaiming the City of God with the barbarians ramping around, Saladin, the noble enemy of Christians, Sir Thomas More, 'the man for all seasons', Sir Humphrey Gilbert calling from the doomed *Squirrel* 'We are as near to

[1] From Longfellow's poem: 'Tell me not in mournful numbers'.

heaven by sea as by land', the great Mogul Emperor, Akbar, discussing religion with a Muslim, a Christian and a Buddhist, Elizabeth Fry penetrating the courts of Europe in her best bonnet that the cry of prisoners might be heard, Seretze Khama, the father of his people, Scott and Wilson awaiting death in the Antarctic with serenity – the gallery seems endless. It is the courage of human-beings that comes over as power for living. Why should we consign a new generation to a world in which none of these people exist?

'And some there be that have no memorial . . . ' Once we are awakened to the reality of this great inhabited past, our imaginations can play also on the memory of those countless nameless ones who fill up the roll of honour. There are also the heroes of endurance as well as action. There is often a feeling, especially among the young, that to suffer things to be done to you is purposeless and humiliating. But history shows the immense dignity of many sufferers from the days of the early Christian martyrs down to the victims of concentration camps in our own day. Indeed, this century has produced as many witnesses to the indomitable force of the human spirit as any, and we have close at hand moving and splendid material in the form of autobiography, war reminiscences and so on.

Of course, as I have already tried to emphasise, the critical element must not be lost. Throughout history people have conducted their struggles from mixed motives, the heroic jostling with curious blends of self-interestedness. In the medieval period the Crusaders offer an excellent opportunity to study some of the paradoxes of human motivation, as we try to understand them wading through the blood of 'unbelievers' to adore the Holy Sepulchre, bickering for leadership or grabbing land, yet convinced that this was a holy war. Too often, we want things in black and white: people and causes should be either right or wrong. History teaches us that life is not like that. Vanity, egotism, self-dramatisation mingle with noble purpose in a Suleiman the Magnificent, a Napoleon, a Nelson or a Gordon. Mixed motives are found in all the great movements for liberation, whether in India, Africa or wherever. This aspect has to be fully and critically explored in any study of great men. I have already suggested that this must not be done in the petty-minded spirit that gleefully cuts them down to ordinary size to prove that we are just as good. Weakness has to be explored as part of the tragedy of the great, not diminishing their greatness but reflecting on the fatal flaws, as, for instance, Shakespeare does in *Macbeth*. In history the most obvious kind of flaw is lust for power and here there opens up a crucial area for discussion in the last year of school. Lord Acton's famous words ('All power corrupts . . . ') still ring in our ears – a cliché, but we see the truth of it every day in our society and in ourselves, in whatever small spheres of power we may have. History should be an education for power because it presents both a warning and a challenge, a warning against self-deception and a challenge to accept responsibility when it comes, in spite of these dangers. A democratic way of life is not to be lived by keeping far from contaminating sources of power but by searching self-criticism and eternal vigilance over those with power.

In one particular respect the way we teach history can have a profound effect on the values which the young carry into their future citizenship. Broad sweeps, generalised outlines, historical 'movements' can produce the notions that the masses, not individuals, have made history, or that people are at the mercy of vast impersonal forces, or that the masses have always been manipulated by demagogues. This leads to a feeling of historical inevitability which, whether articulated or not, paralyses any belief in individual political choice or responsibility for the ordinary citizen. Some would certainly hold that this is a true view, but I should take sides with writers such as Isaiah Berlin who have attacked the concept of historical inevitability as untrue and immoral. When we break up the large movements into the minutiae of actual responses, choices, actions which compose them, we see more clearly that each individual bit of the mosaic has had its necessary place. It is through teaching the particularity of history that we get this across. Many of us would agree that we need future citizens who are not going to be paralysed by the feeling that 'history has us by the throat', and who have learnt that a multitude of individual decisions can add up to a movement of importance. What we do not always realise is that the very way we handle generalisation and particularity in teaching history contains an implicit value judgement for or against historical inevitability.

Another response evoked by the study of history is the passion to get at the truth or as near it as possible. This passion belongs to the true historian and in this sense all young explorers of history of any age can be inspired to be 'true historians'. We begin with the simple question 'How do we know?' and scrutinise our history books to find out what the author's statements are based on. We go on to learn what 'sources' are, how you judge their trustworthiness and what you do when two sources disagree. In one comprehensive school I know, the second-year history course starts with the question What is history? and many other schools, some stimulated by the Schools Council History Project 13-16, follow similar courses. These introduce at once the words 'evidence', 'source', 'document' etc., and different types of history are discussed. It is an exciting experience to reach the point when you can criticise 'what the book says' in the light of your authorities, and it is an education which begins to liberate from the tyranny of the printed word. Though chastened, I could not help being pleased when a budding historian from a junior school wrote to tell me of a mistake I had made in a book he was using. Above all, a young researcher discovers his own critical faculty and power to pursue the truth independently. And looking for the truth in history particularly shows up many things: what we mean by propaganda methods, both crude and subtle, which twist the truth; the meaning of ambiguity and paradox (without necessarily using those words); the different aspects which truth presents when looked at from two different sides. It is hardly necessary to emphasise how important these insights are for present living and our need for a rising generation that can read or listen with a critical eye and ear.

Sometimes the rôle of history may be to make us aware of a new dimension in experience. A friend of mine, teaching in a comprehensive school, sparked off such a moment of new awareness simply by asking the right question. The group was studying primitive man and having a briefing session before visiting a prehistoric site. The question she asked was: 'What do you think made primitive men first think of burying their dead?' Some laughed: it sounded queer. But some days later a big lad stopped the teacher on the stairs: 'It was love', he said. 'What are you talking about?' 'Well, you see, when we were up on that hill, I was imagining two early men hunting a wild beast; it turns and kills one, and the other is just going chasing on with the hunt when he stops and looks at the dead man and feels sorry.' It was, perhaps, that young man's first attempt to articulate what we call a sense of compassion.

Not only can the imaginative experience of history reveal to us a depth of emotion we had not previously realised, as in this last case, but sometimes it gives us the very words in which to express our feelings. We are so often in the position of feeling without being able to articulate fully, and if true feeling lacks adequate expression, human experience is impoverished. One of our first aims in education, of course, is to nourish authentic response in the young in their own authentic personal 'language' (whether in words or some other medium). But where some notable or winged words latch on to our own experience our capacity for self-understanding and therefore self-expression is fed, perhaps through a deeper awareness of the human state, perhaps through a sharper response to beauty, perhaps through a captivating sense of the absurd. Sir Richard Livingstone told the story of a secondary school class, in May, 1941, 'doing Macbeth' rather sleepily because their nights were being badly disturbed by heavy air-raids. Suddenly the words leapt to life and the atmosphere was revitalised when they came to the passage:

> The night has been unruly; where we lay,
> Our chimneys were blown down; and, as they say,

> Lamentings heard i' the air, strange screams of death;
> And prophesying with accents terrible
> Of dire combustion and confused events
> New hatch'd to the woful time; the obscure bird
> Clamour'd the livelong night; some say, the earth
> Was feverous and did shake.

And in spite of the stark tragedy which the words brought back, their sense of the absurd was tickled by 'the obscure bird' which 'clamour'd the livelong night'. That story, of course, is dated, but great literature – and here I unashamedly include literature as history – speaks to many moods and occasions. Sometimes it is the link with personal experience, sometimes the sheer fascination of the words which can make the young (and ouselves) appropriate new language as our own. Some small children, acting the story of Joseph, just enjoyed the words of their incantation as they chanted: 'Bow the knee before the great ruler Zaph-nath-paaneah.' On a quite different level, 'When the morning stars sang together and all the sons of God shouted for joy' catches the very essence of ecstasy on a shining new day or at the pure beginning of all things, while 'What is Man that thou art mindful of him, or the Son of Man that thou visitest him?' has the immensity of the universe as its backcloth. My examples are deliberately Biblical. Many other words from great literature do spontaneously rise out of our hidden memory (if we are reading people) when the occasion sparks them off, but the Biblical ones were once widely used by comparatively unlettered people, and this raises a disturbing question for us today. The Bible in its King James version, and perhaps also, to a lesser extent, the *Pilgrim's Progress*, or for Catholics, the liturgy and certain devotional prayers, were treasure-houses of language for generations of ordinary folk who, whether they could read or not, poured out their feelings about the human condition, its transience, its need for compassion and brotherhood, its dependence on the Creator and its need for salvation in historic words that they had so completely absorbed from their religion as to make their own. It is puzzling to see what the modern equivalent could be and I am tempted to say – without frivolity – that it might be the words and music of pop songs which, though incomparably more shallow, do sometimes express human feelings quite hauntingly. Alas – is the gap between the present experience of the young and the great literature of the past now too wide for the spark to leap across? If this were really so it would be an irreparable tragedy. Why should the languages of great beauty, great profundity or even great absurdity be locked-up treasures, available only to a literary élite? There is a hint of irony here in the fact that the age of universal education may possibly be evolving into the age of non-readers. I think my conviction is that if we really know the 'great words' for ourselves, and make the right links through experience the sparks *will* fly over. I believe that the young in any condition can enrich their self-understanding and powers of communication by appropriating these treasures of the past. Sometimes it can be just the magic of the words themselves that works the trick, and here it is worth observing that if we give them writing-practice there is no need to set nasty little trivial sentences when there are splendid ones close at hand.

Calamity can still strike individuals, families and communities. For all our cushioning devices today, we in Britain are still at the mercy of disaster, violence and sudden death, while in the world as a whole famine and plague still stalk abroad and earthquakes still strike. It is a false view of life to avoid confronting the reality of death. History draws us into the experience of many people in their manner of facing danger and death. A recent book in the Then and There series on the Black Death points this up. The author begins by calling it a horror story and, indeed, it might be said that the first reason for giving the young such a gloomy book is that they revel in the macabre. But the writer's purpose goes deeper:

> The Black Death happened over six hundred years ago and we shall never know exactly how many people died ... But it is not so difficult to understand the feelings of people at the time, to share the grief on Wednesday of a child whose father had died on Monday and his mother on Tuesday. It is easy to sympathise with those who tried to run away, to admire those who stayed and tried to help the dying. I hope you will never have to face the kind of disaster that struck the people living in the fatal year of 1348 but it is no good pretending that something equally horrible could not happen to all of us in our lifetime. It could, and even if it was a much lesser disaster like a car crash happening to one of your friends, studying and thinking about what the Black Death did to people could help you to understand what people feel and how they behave at bad moments in their lives.[1]

Here is a piece of history which brings home some of the depths of tragedy in the lives of ordinary people and calls on the reader to enter in imagination into precisely *this* kind of human experience. Less dramatically, graveyards, those quiet repositories of history, give us not only elegies but case-histories on dying. If we teach in a village or town where there are still old graveyards around churches or chapels, a study of gravestones, their designs, inscriptions, family details and so on, can illuminate our social history uniquely, looking at it, perhaps, *sub specie eternitatis*. There, family history is told in a few words and attitudes towards death can be read in symbols, texts and

[1] D. Turner, *The Black Death*, Then and There series, Longman, 1978, pp. 5-6.

other quotations – even sometimes with a wry humour coming through. Death, then, is a part of the human condition which we ought not to evade. After a class discussion had turned on to the question of death, some boys said to their teacher (a visiting one): 'Miss, you haven't seen our churchyard.' They seized her by the arms and insisted on taking her there after school. On the way it became evident that they wanted to talk about this great unspoken fear of theirs. In the graveyard their usual rather rough voices and manners were sloughed off: they stepped round the graves carefully and knelt down to try and decipher inscriptions and symbols. It was, in fact, a very good reading lesson for them and they had wanted to show off their reading, but, much more, in this quiet mood they were linking themselves to their past folk and learning something about themselves in the process.

On a more objective level, a group can find out much about past living and dying by gathering data from gravestones. Statistics on infant mortality, for instance, or the death-rate among young adults, can be most revealing, bringing home sharply the closeness of early death in families of the past compared with our much longer natural expectation of life today. Making rubbings of the better preserved inscriptions leads to a study of religious symbols and their meanings and why people in the past found certain texts and symbols the most comforting. Language work can be sparked off by Latin quotations which often point up the Latin root of English words (for example *Miles Christi*). In the course of this work we can get over the point that the solemn context in which this historical material is placed is not morbid but realistic. A recent appealer for volunteers to clean up a neglected graveyard announced: 'Your one chance to mingle with the great!' Our graveyards may not be thronged with the great, but it would be good if a project on gravestones evoked the impulse to honour the past by such a cleaning-up labour, where it is needed.

Finally, interwoven like a thread through all histories of all tribes and nations in all ages, is the 'long search' of men for their meaning and their destiny – in religious terms, for God. The reality of this as a valid theme in history has been, and still is, under attack, yet in that procession of heroes we glanced at, most, if not all, believed that God was the basis of their power. Moreover, many signs suggest that today this 'search' is still real as a part of our consciousness. This means that the spiritual history of mankind in the past is of great importance in the present. For every search has a past. In strengthening the rising generation for their own quest, we must supply nourishment from the experience of many witnesses in many ages and many faiths who were pilgrims 'seeking a city'.

Although I fear it may be obscure, this chapter has really been about the kind of responses which history can inspire. For, although it must be tempered by the critical mind, the heart is as important as the head. Most surprisingly, researchers in a recent Harvard project on Technology, Work and Character have reached the conclusion that the business executive must find his heart:

> Only a well-developed heart can invest information with spiritual weight. It takes a well-developed heart to make difficult judgements in terms of the human values involved.[1]

Here, from an unexpected quarter, is support for the experience of history as a necessary part of education. My argument has been that deepening our awareness of all the complex facets of human motive and behaviour, as seen in history, heightens our powers to live our own lives with perception, feeling and energy. If we are tempted today in the West to drift trivially on the moment because we hope we are cushioned against disaster, history teaches us otherwise. The great realities of living and dying are still the same. Our present condition calls as ever for the dimensions of commitment, heroic struggle, enthusiasm, endurance, faithfulness, compassion, as well as the will to search for the truth unflinchingly and the power to use power properly. It demands that we seek to make a responsible impact on life, that we find worthy language in which to share our experience, and that we confront death steadfastly. Tragedy is a built-in element in the human situation and, paradoxically, part of its glory. The experience of history will not let us evade either death or tragedy: they confront us there on a grand scale. Yet the last word here must be on enjoyment. Even the tragedy of history is to be 'enjoyed', perhaps in the sense of Greek catharsis. To be swept by the power of imaginative sympathy into these other realms is an enjoyment in its own right. Because it is so, it helps to generate a sense of significance in all human existence, the power to cope with our here and now, and vision to work towards an ever-new future shape of things to come.

[1] M. Maccoby, 'The Corporate Climber has to find his heart', *Fortune*, December, 1976.

5
Communicating history

1 Selecting topics

What are we trying to transmit as we teach? There are many levels in teaching. It may be that we are training in skills or handing out usefully packaged information for practical purposes. These processes have their appropriate techniques and relationships. But communicating history, as we have seen, is an attempt to draw learners of whatever age into a human experience. Almost by definition, therefore, we must be 'inside' that experience ourselves. We shall transmit little or nothing – no spark will run between teller and listener, leader and explorers – unless we believe in that experience ourselves and want to share it. That is the first and fundamental principle in teaching history – indeed, any of the humanities.

But of course, for the young to enter into that 'territory' its theme or themes must be appropriate to the level of their own experience: a child of ten would have to be precocious to be able to sit down in imagination at the Versailles Peace Conference in 1919 and enter fully into the issues at stake. So the second principle is to use our imaginations to understand what our particular age group are likely to be able to appropriate as their own and what they cannot. Syllabus-making has to be governed not by 'what they ought to know' but by what they can appropriate and therefore enjoy. The main consideration here lies in the question of motifs or themes. What types of human feeling and activity are intelligible at various ages? We have already touched on a number of motifs which come naturally to various ages of primary school children: exploration, hidden treasure or detective work, playing at primitive life, rôle play in basic jobs – all these gain ready entry into their imaginative experience. How men first discovered or invented things we take for granted (uses of fire, pottery, weaving, writing, the wheel and so on) add wonder to the everyday environment. Warfare, we must face it, is also a natural motif for children, as witness all the small boys who run about sputtering like machine guns or yelling with their tomahawks. We should not evade this aspect of conflict through the ages, but let them work out strategy and tactics, methods of attack and defence evolving weapons and machines of war as their interest dictates. Gradually the bloody tragedy of war may be perceived or can be presented to them and the fundamental point of the price paid for heroic glory in battle can be pressed home. Later, as adolescent students, we can consider with them the great human predicament presented by T. S. Eliot's starkly realistic question:

Do you think . . . that lions no longer need keepers?

If the motifs are right, strange ways of life can be enjoyed. I once spent several weeks with eight-year-olds in the ancient Egypt of our imagination. We could do this because the main theme was Joseph and his brethren and quarrelling families were only too familiar to all of us. Indeed, our first attempts at free-acting the opening scene descended at once to the level of Camberwell street-quarrelling and could have gone on so for hours. Then one child discovered that the story was in the Bible. We made her chief scribe with the duty of reading out bits. They loved the language and it was fascinating to watch how their own language elevated itself: when they came to the ritual of Pharaoh's court they were ready to play Joseph in all his grandeur. I have already quoted one of their ritual chants. In the meantime they had learnt quite a bit about the civilisation of ancient Egypt, its domestic life, art, religion, writing and so on. They were particularly delighted at the idea of wearing cones of nard on their heads at a feast to supply the oil needed in that hot climate. But we did not, at this stage, concern ourselves with problems of historicity or period: this was simply the adventures of a boy and his brothers, a moving story which we could understand, acted against a strange and exciting background.

So the main consideration in choosing topics is that the core of the action should be intelligible in the motives and feelings that inspired it. This is really Collingwood's 'inside of the fact' again, and it is more important than the 'outside', however dramatic that might chance to be. For instance, in spite of its thriller quality, I do not think the story of Becket is appropriate in the primary school, where it has so often appeared, because to treat it simply as a story of two quarrelling men with a murder at the end is to vulgarise it. Not until something of the principles behind the clash between Church and State can be grasped is this topic appropriate. Similarly, the complexities of politics intertwined in the story of Henry VIII and his wives or of Elizabeth I and Mary, Queen of Scots put these, in my view, outside the range of the primary school, however much the more dramatic bits (as sometimes vulgarised by the mass media) may appeal. But my point about Becket once elicited the riposte: 'But what about children living in Canterbury?' 'Well yes', one had to reply, 'then it becomes a part of knowing your own world.' In choosing topics local associations can sometimes make relevant themes which otherwise would not 'hook on' at all.

At the secondary level, I suggest, the same motifs are often appropriate in the first two years at least, but the material has to be more sophisticated in form and, progressively, motives and feelings have to be explored in greater depth. Love, hate, fear, hero-worship, awe and pity are emotions that the young are beginning to discover in themselves. They can therefore be invited to examine and reflect on other people's feelings and in so doing come to understand more about their own. I have already discussed in some detail the problem of how we handle British history, economic and political, at the secondary level. Although, as I have argued, some governmental problems such as finance and justice can best be grasped first of all at the simpler level of medieval kingship, the great themes of modern British and world history can surely be handled, provided they are treated thematically and actualised within the theme, rather than being rattled off in rapid chronological succession. It is easy to make a list in abstract terms – the spread of Islam, the growth of Parliament, the evolution of the British Cabinet, the Irish Question, British Imperialism, the rise of African Nationalism, the making of Modern China, and so forth – but to explore motives, the actions of people within institutional frameworks, the workings of power, attention has to be focused on actual people at actual moments thinking, feeling, saying and doing in specific ways. I remember a school certificate paper which was in danger of getting no marks at all because the learnt notes had so manifestly been unintelligible. Then suddenly there was a break-through on a question which involved the Gold Rush to Australia. Breathlessly the candidate plunged in: 'And my great-grandfather went to Australia for gold', and he did this and he did that – a whole page of family experience which earned ten marks as authentic history. Sometimes, indeed, the gap between present experience and what seems a proper syllabus is too great. A class of girls, school-leavers mostly, were ostensibly 'doing' Walpole, and the 'sleeping dogs' were indeed just lying: manifestly they were miles away. When asked what they wanted to do after leaving school they nearly all answered: 'Hairdressing.' A project on hairdressing through the ages sparked them off in a way that the evolution of Cabinet Government never would have, and at least they departed with their own picture of successive civilisations expressed in their styles of hair and clothes.

I shall be turning a little later to the problem of the abstract vocabulary of history but here let me quote Vivian Galbraith, a distinguished historian of English administrative history. 'All history is an attempt to understand the feelings and the thoughts of folk in the past.'[1] To give 'body' to political history we have constantly to be operating 'inside' the events, lest misunderstandings arise because we did not tease out the full action. The same kind of issue arises even more acutely in connection with world history courses. We tend to think in terms of 'great movements' and it is precisely this concept which puts up a barrier against the imagination, because it seems tacitly to subordinate individual people, their choices and their actions, to vast impersonal forces. I have already argued that it is dangerous thinking to over-emphasise great sweeps of happening in which the masses are caught as victims. Hence, once more, we need to select themes where the material really does exist to actualise situations in some detail and to dissect who took decisions and how and by whom power was actually operated.

This leads directly to my next principle of syllabus-making: topics should be chosen where there is sufficient rich and satisfying detail available to supply answers to as many questions as possible and to afford an exciting field of 'research' to the questers. A characteristic of the adult historical mind is, I think, that we select 'aspects' which we define by artificial rather than natural boundaries, designed to give us a tolerably limited area in which to work. Thus we may well choose to study some aspect of feudalism rather than the total life of a feudal family, or Queen Elizabeth's diplomacy, George III's concept of kingship, Gladstone and the Irish Question, rather than any of these 'in the round'. The reason is obvious, and I remember a student who complained about the difficulty of reading Sir Maurice Powicke on the thirteenth century precisely because he did see people in the round and would go off in the midst of discussing a baron's relations with Henry III to put his wife and children and his wife's ramifications into the picture. What we forget is that children are not yet burdened with this sense that one must discard in order to make learning manageable and tolerable. They want to know everything about someone, and, of course, soak it up like blotting-paper. A story, brought to what we think to be a nice artistic conclusion, is greeted by the question: 'But what did they do next?' They want to imagine these people whole: dressing, eating and playing, making houses, living through tomorrow. If the sources are poor or difficult they are disappointed. But there are so many, both ancient and modern, with amazing and curious detail on human behaviour and increasingly

[1] V. Galbraith, *Domesday Book: Its Place in Administrative History*, Clarendon Press, 1974, p. 170.

such source material is available in easy form. Indeed, this point about detail has really caught on with publishers: there has been a small revolution in the move from text-books to topic-books for which vivid detail from source material of all kinds has been garnered and brought together with loving care.[1] The riches found in the tomb of Tutankamun, the abandoned shops of Pompeii, a medieval recipe for a 'great pie' or the procession bringing in the boar's head, Queen Elizabeth I's three hundred and sixty-five dresses, the way tobacco was grown in Virginia, the splendour and squalor of the palace at Versailles, barbarian Englishmen in Peking or cowboys in the Middle West – a list of the colourful and curious could be endless.[2] There is ample treasure to be discovered, sometimes visually, sometimes in written sources, although, of course, not all questions will find answers. As against the 'aspects' of adult history, the principle of unity for the young is, I think, that of actors against a full background: scene by scene they want the action in all its encompassing detail.

Studying people in this way takes time, so my final principle is to select few enough topics for the year to spend at least several weeks, if not half a term, on each. Of necessity, however, this principle can only be applied in primary classes and pre-public-examination classes in secondary schools. This question of taking enough time relates not only to the need to build a detailed and rounded picture, but also to the questions of language and activity which we shall discuss later. But taking time is not consistent with the concept of outlines, and so we reach the controversy of Outlines versus Patches. The case for outlines really stems from the concept of an ordered, schematised historical framework into which facts everyone ought to know are slotted. You may later retain nothing but the hard little facts, but at least you can put them in the right period and, with luck, date them. There is perhaps (or was) a point in starting out with this kind of equipment. It was put in an early nineteenth-century letter of a mother to her eight-year-old son:

Letter from Anne Whitaker to her son, Alfred, 20 September, 1805:

Do you continue to read the English History – I wish you to be well acquainted with it – there is scarcely any species of ignorance that will let a Man down in Company than an ignorance of Geography and History, particularly that of his own Country.

---

[1] See chapter 8 for detailed suggestions on topics.
[2] One of these series has been the Then and There series with which I have been closely associated since 1954 when the first title was published. Many of the examples of topics chosen throughout the book inevitably come from that series.

Even in these more casual days it is useful to know what the Fourth of July means to Americans or Bastille Day to the French. But this collection of little facts is not the experience of history as we have been thinking of it. The thin outline course can only really be appropriated by students who already have experienced the 'inside' of enough historical situations to enable them to fill in some detail of what lies within the dehydrated statements confronting them. I once had an argument with an external examiner in a college of education who maintained that the less advanced students could only cope with outlines. 'On the contrary', said I, 'Outlines can only be assimilated by the more advanced or able; to understand what it is all about, the weaker ones first need detailed, fully expounded topics. Don't spread the butter thinly all over; give it to them in lumps.' Actually, a compromise can be made: topics can be taken in their proper historical sequence and even linked by connecting threads. To change the metaphor, this gives us a kind of thin historical string with fat beads strung along it at intervals.

But the fat beads are the most important – or rather, to revert to my original metaphor – the patches. Patch history has now become quite a term of art. I think its origin was in a discussion about history in the BBC Schools Council in the late nineteen-forties. I said: 'I want children to sit down in a good rich patch of history and stay there for a satisfying amount of time.' To which the chief officer of the council, Richard Steele, replied: 'So what you want is Patch History.' The pure patch method is in some ways the most satisfying, because it embodies most clearly the concept of actors against their background and demands unity of time and place: unity of time defined, perhaps as the life-time of one group of actors, or less; unity of place, as one city, village or region. But of course there have to be many compromises, for even a syllabus composed on patch lines must sometimes cover wider ground. The story of a family over several generations can supply the principle of unity, or even the life-history of a city. Where the time-span has to be long, several close-up foci can give body, forming a miniature string with several beads on it. Thus a topic on Mohammed must carry the story several centuries beyond his death; one on Ancient Rome at the secondary level must have at least two foci, Republican and Imperial Rome. Europe in the eighteenth century, seen through the eyes of the travelling Boswell, has unity of time in the person of the main actor, but not unity of place. This topic illustrates very well, however, the use of successive close-ups to convey a broad scene: instead of a survey of abstracted statements covering 'the rise of Prussia', 'Austria under Maria Theresa', 'France in the eighteenth century' et al., we can have a series of vivid vignettes in which the reactions of the main actor turn all the abstractions into human terms.

There are, however, threads as well as patches – not just the thin threads of time by which we connect our detailed studies, but broader ones of themes to be traced through several centuries or right through the ages. Merchant Adventurers in the East is an example of such a theme in which the difficulty of coping in the imagination with the extensive time-span is balanced by the easy intelligibility of the main motif. For primary schools there are all the evolutionary themes related to everyday life, such as the history of sign languages, writing and other means of communication, houses through the ages, the evolution of transport or tools. Here the concreteness or practical purpose of the subject material is what the children lay hold of. The long passage of time is less important at this stage than the sequence of change or progress. Egyptians and their writing are hardly further off than their grandmothers who, if they are dead, are themselves already 'a long time ago'. Time is relative, but the histories of successive discovery, invention, adaptation, progress, convey the important notion of change through time. At the secondary level themes of change and progress can be more technical in dealing with the material environment and also introduce some of the history of ideas, such as are embodied in the development of medicine or of science in general, or in such themes as the growth of toleration.

I have discussed the selection of topics as if we were just teachers of history operating each in our own little tight circle, but, in fact, it is self-evident that many or all historical topics can sweep almost the whole curriculum into one basket: geography, literature, science, music, art, movement and so on and so on. If an integrated studies programme is fully adopted, for 'history teacher' one should read 'team teacher', since the rich fields of such topics can best be explored under a team of guides with differing expertise. I have also written as if we had only to devise a single programme for a class group. On the contrary, there are many possible patterns of work, with individual or sub-group projects going on within, or alongside, or even instead of, main group work. But whatever the organisation, principles for selecting 'good topics' remain, I believe, the same.

2 Introducing topics

We have moved a long way from the 'talk and chalk' principle of teaching. The latest ideas put all the emphasis on individual initiative and discovery. School children sitting in rows listening appear at the far end of a scale which has moved right over to Open Plan teaching at the other end. Are we in danger of moving too far? Perhaps the prevailing influence in this movement has been modern educational psychology which has taught us to respect and cherish the individual creativity of the young and this has coincided with the pervasive mood of uncertainty which has infected adults in Western liberal societies. Just as we shrink from the patriarchal image in the family, so we abhor the teacher-dominated class, but if one side of the educational coin is individual freedom, the other side is relationship, and they are one coin. We grow through living relationships with other persons. I have emphasised that history is such an experience of relating oneself to people in the past, but they need very careful introductions. They do not just meet us in the street. The grand vocation of a teacher of history is to effect these introductions. But they have to be introductions with power – the power of our own delight. As a rule we can only introduce effectively people to whom we have related ourselves and whom we want our pupils to know. I remember once listening to a student introducing Clive of India to a class. Clearly, Clive lighted no spark in him and the result was complete indifference, not only to Clive's adventures, but to the whole fascinating scene of India. Now you might have reservations about Clive himself, but to treat the millions of a great people with indifference is a sin against humanity. Today that student would probably not get away with it. A teacher dare not appear bored: if he is not really 'inside' the story he must at least get up some spurious excitement.

Thus in many cases, though not all, the first steps into a new topic of history must be taken on the initiative of the teacher. The feet will not usually move into the new territory unless activated by an impelling introduction. Impelling words can be in the form of a tantalisingly brief introduction with just enough detail to whet the appetite and then a winged question with a barb to strike home and rouse the explorer or detective instinct, but, as I have already argued, do not let us forget the time-honoured 'straight' narrative. Verbal story-telling is as ancient as man's memory: is it now outmoded?

Some would say emphatically 'yes'. Films, television programmes, colour transparencies, tapes and so on can be so good, with all the resources of expertise and technical equipment at the command of those who produce them, that few ordinary teachers can compete. The young, too, are conditioned to learning from pictures, symbols and sounds, rather than from words. The long age of word-dominated education is over and now the initial approach to a new topic, so the argument runs, must be through some audio-visual set piece. This view does make a valid point: for centuries the tradition of Western education was almost wholly literary and mathematical, with little appeal to visual imagery or sound, and when education was extended to the masses the same model dictated the rigid concentration on the 'three Rs'. Today the widening of the concept of communication in education to embrace the 'languages' of the visual arts, music and the dance has been greatly enriching. Yet when this is said, I think the present time asks of us two resolutions in education: not to let the power of purely verbal communication go by default, that is, by lack of practice; not to abandon the direct rôle of the teacher as the communicator, with or without the support of some audio-visual resource. The first finds its justification in the store-houses of literary beauty which, without some effort, may become inaccessible to very many of the young today. Studying *Romeo and Juliet* solely from the screen is no substitute for reading at least some of the text together in a group. The second rests on a belief in the power of direct personal relationship in the schoolroom. The teacher is there in the flesh, not remotely operating on the screen; his (or her) involvement in the subject can be directly observed; above all, he or she can be immediately questioned, or can reply at once to various kinds of comment or reaction. Probably it is true that, in general, live story-telling is still a vital teaching method in the primary school, but that at the secondary stage it has to be used more sparingly. Mixed ability groups are more difficult, at this age, to hold together and often seem happiest when working on their own assignments. Yet even here there are themes which demand verbal narrative to convey high drama, a pathetic or tragically moving story, or even great horror. The heroism and tragedy of Scott's last journey needs more than screen pictures to get across the struggles, the sacrificial comradeship, the end – so near to safety. Broadcast talks by no means always have the right vocabulary and tone of voice; moreover, however good, I am not sure that they can always make the full impact that a teacher in the classroom, moved himself by the story, can make.

I have often asked myself what makes good oral communication, and listened to a variety of speakers to try and discover. It is not just a question of the usual rules of good speaking, though these, of course, are useful. It is much more a matter of the unspoken communication going on between the speaker and listener. First, there is a kind of anticipatory gleam in the eye of the narrator which conveys the sense that you have something to share which you have enjoyed. Then there is the sense of immediacy: this is not just a story which you prepared last night and have in your notes, but something that is immediately in the forefront of your mind and imagination *now*. I once listened to a lecturer, known for his capacity to 'hold an audience', when he was speaking on a remote and erudite theme, the road system in the ancient Middle East. By no means all his student audience were specialising in this field but all were completely absorbed because at the moment of speaking he was in imagination travelling along those ancient desert tracks himself. To involve the listeners one has first to be involved oneself, re-creating step by step, as it proceeds, the whole narrative. Immediacy, involvement, imagination – these are the keys to the narrative that really does transport from here to there. Although some are born story-tellers and some are not, we should all, I think, if we teach at all, be able to communicate what we believe to be worthwhile and enjoyable in this way.

This sense of worth, this conviction that our material is of intrinsic value is all-important. 'History is about chaps'; chaps are people; the greatest value, perhaps, that our society needs to learn today is the value of people. So let us not throw off millions of chaps by the wayside as we march our students, with cheerful or uncheerful indifference, through the centuries. We should all be alert today to the wrong-ness of 'teaching the British Empire' jingoistically, but do we realise that to teach it with indifference to the fate of tribes and peoples is equally wrong? To teach any great theme in history with indifference is to trivialise it and this does violence to human life. Our Victorian forefathers drew their moral lessons at the end of the story. This is not our style, but by the sympathy and imagination with which we draw out the story, the moral is made: that people rising to heroism or disintegrating into terror or evil, people toiling for a livelihood and governing their societies, people living and people dying are of great value.

3 Using historical language

One way of measuring the march of civilisation is by growth in the use of abstraction and generalisation. Men observed the recurrence of phenomena and the repetition of patterns and evolved the language in which to pack up much in little and to draw conclusions without spelling everything out. Certainly the writing of history would have been impossible without the development of such language. What should we do without such words as policy, administration, organisation, development, influence, process and the like? But this vocabulary can become a jargon that deadens perception, almost enslaves. The clichés flow from the pen or the tongue in a stream that drowns the imagination. A fresh and vivid turn of phrase in a history book delights because of its unexpected sharpness. Whatever the usefulness of the vocabulary of professional history, it can dull our sense of the immense realities of human affairs, because we can so easily write them off in clichés. Consider a few common phrases: 'the policy was successful'; 'the campaign was vigorously pursued'; 'his influence was waning'; 'the persecution of heretics went on unrelentingly'. Maybe as we write them our imagination can play over the variety of activities, struggles, hopes, fears and sufferings packed up in these glib phrases, but our readers and listeners may very well not have the equipment to fill all this in. For them history may be just a matter of abstracted statements remote from real life.

Adults are conditioned to live, perhaps too much, among large abstractions: the modern state spawns them at every turn. Children and young people are not to be caught this way. If the vocabulary in which human happenings are presented is not direct and vivid, it will not take hold. If pressurised, they can learn off the jargon correctly enough to pass examinations but the clichés may mean nothing. So, whether speaking or writing, we have to struggle for a freshly-minted vocabulary. That it is a struggle is evident from the work of many writers of school history books who fall into the cliché bog without even noticing it and sometimes never get out. I suggest there are some guide lines we can follow. First of all, for ages up to about thirteen or fourteen we should, as a rule, eschew altogether the kind of abstract words named in the last paragraph. One could make a list of some twenty proscribed words. Until their own experience and widening knowledge of human affairs gives some content to them, the young cannot 'use' these words, though they may well be able to spell, pronounce and put them in writing. I remember myself being secretly puzzled about the real *content* of the word 'administration' for years after I could put it correctly into an essay. Again, take the word 'policy': what is it but a series of thoughts, decisions, actions, taken by one or more persons in a particular situation, but how impossible to give an illuminating definition of it to someone who cannot yet mentally picture this process going on.

Secondly, when the time comes to introduce them, we must handle these abstract words and phrases as portmanteau expressions which have a lot packed up inside themselves. The need then is to unpack the portmanteaus. Once again we see that this takes much more time. Instead of rattling off 'The Treaty of Versailles was signed in . . .', we have to re-create in imagination something of the setting, the to-ing and fro-ing of diplomats, their bargaining and the final signing ceremony. In bringing to actuality some of these great occasions dramatic and documentary programmes on television have been a great asset, giving visual and aural embodiment to what otherwise can remain dead words. But history books are still littered with these portmanteau statements and until we have unpacked them they make no impact because they strike no bell in the imagination. It is not their difficulty in spelling or pronunciation that forms the real barrier, but their cloudiness of meaning. New words are a delight to the young, but what they seize hold of initially are concrete words – the proper technical terms for weapons, tools, armour, clothes, food, machines and the like. It is probably only in the secondary stage that we can start to introduce them to many abstractions. A good test of suitability at any stage is how easily we can provide an intelligible definition, without walking all round the shop, when asked 'what does that word mean?' Quite often dictionary definitions will not do and we have to compose (with the class) special glossaries. Original source work provides a good way into this expanding language work, for if it is an exciting or intriguing piece, the incentive to master words is there. What is inadmissible (but so easy to do) is to take refuge ourselves in 'dead words' because we cannot think up any better ones.

Another guideline is to eschew the impersonal or passive voice as far as we can. It is amazing how circumlocutory historians can be (and others, for I recently read an amusing article which was a tirade against the tyranny of the passive voice over scientists). 'It was thought fit to'; 'it was decided that'; 'the battle was won by'; 'reform was proposed' – the list could be endless. If you count up the number of impersonal and passive verbs on a page of an average history book, the result can be surprising. Sometimes passiveness is combined with abstractness: 'the situation improved slowly but the trouble had a lasting effect': where are the *people* in that sentence? Again, such and such an institution 'stood for every form of oppression and little was done to ease the position'. What troubles and sufferings are effectively concealed behind the following: 'Clothing and ammunition were short because of corruption and mismanagement'? Instead of circumlocution it is the direct, active, crisp statement that we need: 'their threat was carried out' can become 'they actually did this'; 'X was responsible for drawing up this law' can be 'X made this law'; 'few families were able to have more than one room' = 'most families lived in one room'; 'the council consisted of x men' = 'they chose x men for the council'; 'it was seen to contain' = 'people found in it'. Another of our habits as historians is to use 'concealed metaphors'. I call them concealed because they have become so much a part of our jargon that we are no longer aware of them as metaphors. But to a literal-minded boy or girl phrases like 'he took steps to procure', 'he threw caution to the winds', 'the policy broke down', 'they dug up an old quarrel', can leave a confused, cloudy impression because just that much removed from a plain statement of what actually happened. A girl, sent to the headmaster to be disciplined, came back looking really frightened. 'He said he would keep the sentence hanging over my head', she told her teacher. 'Did he really mean *hanging*?' Another story of literal-mindedness is appropriate here. I was once marking a batch of School Certificate papers in which it was fairly clear that the group might not be highly intelligent, but had learnt their notes on nineteenth-century British history very conscientiously. They were all passing but I wondered how much they really understood. And then in an answer on the repeal of the Corn Laws, the lid came off when a candidate wrote: 'And Robert Peel lost his seat because he was late and someone else got it first.'

The criteria, then, for good historical language seem to me to be directness, simplicity, use of active verbs, vivid description of concrete objects and specific actions, straight expression of emotions. When we reach the stage of introducing abstract expressions they must be given real content. It occurs to me that it would sharpen our own awareness of the meaning of words and illuminate them for our older pupils if we took a little while to look at the derivations of words we often use. Five minutes with Skeat's *Concise Etymological Dictionary of the English Language* (my edition is OUP, 1961) produces the following fascinating examples:

administer, administration: from the Latin verb *ministrare*, to serve.
develop, development: related to its opposite *envelop*, both probably derived from the Teutonic *lap*, to wrap, hence to develop = to unwrap.
influence: same root as influenza, from the Latin verb *influere*, to flow in.
organise, organisation: from the Greek *organon*, an implement to work with.
operate, operation: from the Latin verb *operare*, to work.
policy: from the Greek *polis*, a city, a state.
process: from the Latin verb *procedere*, *processum*, to go forward (same as procession).
relate, relationship: from the Latin verb *referre*, *relatum*, to refer or carry back to.
situation: from the Latin verb *situare*, to place.
communicate, communication: has a particularly illuminating root: from the Latin *com (cum)*, together with, and *munis*, ready to serve.

Notice how many of these words seem to move from a practical activity expressed in a verb to a theoretical concept. To track their paths backwards almost peoples them with nameless persons doing things long ago.

In many ways the instinct of the young for direct statement is sound. In setting out to communicate with them in language that really makes an impact, we are not 'talking down' but quite often trying to make a salutary escape from the meshes of our over-abstracted and cliché-ridden language. But all the same, the vocabulary of abstraction and generalisation remains with us: it is too useful to eschew. This book is written in it, although it would probably be better if rid of its jargon!

6
Understanding history through activity

To understand is to respond, for gaining understanding is never a passive process. (It is, of course, a different thing from acquiring packages of information which you retain for examination purposes and then throw away). No learning is complete without some activity of body, mind or imagination. The old joke about transferring what is in the teacher's notes to the pupil's without the subject-matter passing through the mind of either pin-points neatly what understanding is *not*. The immediate response to a stirring story or a door-opening question is a kindling of the imagination; the next, a desire to 'do something about it' for yourself. One of the splendid things that has happened in our schools, largely, though not entirely, since the Second World War, is the great 'activity revolution'. Go into almost any school and the fruits are all around you in puppets and pictures, dashing displays and ambitious models. Here a group may be recording their own television programme or taping their play, there individuals may be creating their own books from their own project material, or again, a group is expressing some theme in literature or history in mime and movement. The whole gamut of activities is being explored and the school hums like a busy hive. The last thing I would want to do in this chapter is to tell teachers about what they are already doing. But perhaps, when the pace is often breathless, there is need for occasional reflection on why we stimulate this or that activity and what educational achievements can result. To begin with, one general reflection occurs to me: what a fruitful *social* experience history (and literature) can provide! Making large constructions (for example, a castle, an Elizabethan theatre, or a model of old London Bridge) can obviously be cooperative. Dramatisation at all levels is so by its very nature, drawing in hand-workers and artists as well as actors. Puppet shows as splendid social activities hardly need to be mentioned. But the sharing can go beyond the producing group. Models and exhibitions can be shown to other groups in the school and the onus to share, not only what you have enjoyed finding out about and making, but a clear explanation of what it all means fosters good communication at an expository level, whether oral or written.

Drama, when it has moved beyond spontaneous play, demands an audience, and an audience can be critical as well as appreciative. I lately saw in a junior department criticisms by an older group of a puppet show presented by the youngest group: they were very socially aware documents, kind, encouraging, but firmly and tactfully critical at points.

Perhaps we should place first, especially for the primary school, the instant physical response that some stories evoke. Children playing at hunters or jousting knights at the lists are instantly embodying their imaginative understanding in movement. I remember some nine-year-olds being introduced to Livingstone in the African jungle. Because they only knew smooth London parks, we imagined what it would be like to be pushing through grass and undergrowth higher than yourself. The next step was to try and feel in their own muscles this exploration through the long grass. Of course today they would probably know visually what a jungle was like from television but getting the feel in your bones is no less an instinctive response. Again, I have seen young children solemnly taking possession of the child-size castle they had built and pulling up the drawbridge behind them. At a more sophisticated level come the mimes and dances in which all the emotions of different human situations can be studied and given body. Thus in a junior class I have seen a mime of Guy Fawkes to seventeenth-century music in which conspiracy, cunning, stealth, fear, *vox populi* and retributive justice all descended from their abstract stations to be embodied by young actors.

Then there is the sharp dart of curiosity which quickens the impulse to find out more and gives the young their first taste of the analytical method. Questions dissect the field of exploration. Younger children compile lists of what they want to find out, each egging the others on to think of more questions, until the list is perforce closed and the questions can be sorted out into categories (in adult parlance), such as food, clothes, houses. Older groups use, perhaps, larger or more subtle categories, but for all learning through asking questions and dissecting information, in other words, through analysis, is an important experience. Not only is the information broken up, but for the time being the group itself often breaks up into sub-groups or even individual researchers. This type of work has, of course, proved particularly valuable in mixed ability groups. Worksheets devised at varying levels to meet differing needs are now a commonplace, but we must be clear that if the teacher prepares them, half the analysis is already done, whereas a programme of things to discover which has been worked out by the young themselves is training them to investigate *ab initio*.

The young researcher today quite often finds a feast of intriguing material spread for him. School libraries (even in these penurious days) carry a range of the new-style topic books, public libraries expect to be used as guides, local museums open up their treasures. To see the young at work, examining objects and pictures, searching the indices of books, consulting encyclopedias, making notes and drawings in answer to their own questions, brings home the sense that the 'insatiable curtiosity' (*sic*) of the human animal can early become a driving force of intellectual development. And one of the first intellectual discoveries can be the crucial distinction between primary and secondary sources. They will probably have begun with some of the attractive books now written for them but with the right stimulus they can soon get behind these with the question: How did the writer know this was so? So they move on to nose out all they can from original material. The easiest kind of clue often lies in artefacts or pictures of the period. These contemporary objects are not extra frills or a little extra jam to make the all-important 'word' more digestible. On the contrary, they are 'words' to be studied in their own right. To examine and draw or model a flint arrowhead or Roman lamp with the care it deserves brings the distant past right into our hands and is an education in itself. Again, modern photography opens up great riches in film-strips, book illustrations and television. An immense wealth of absorbing detail is laid open to us, for instance, in medieval manuscripts or Elizabethan pictures. (Incidentally, the word manu-script – written by hand – itself invites attention, opening up the pre-printing press world.) Sources which can be 'read' directly with the eye give an immediate meeting with history and a concrete meaning to the word 'source'.

To digress for a moment here on pictures, it seems that we still have to press the case against 'made-up' pictures, that is, the modern artist's re-creation of a scene. The case is two-fold. First, if the picture is intended, as it should be, to be used as an integral part of the text, that is, to be 'read' for information, it is obvious that it should be an authentic contemporary representation. Secondly, if the picture is merely added as a 'frill', a romantic re-creation which may (or may not) be pleasant on the eye, there is far more sense in giving the readers the ingredients (buildings, clothes etc.) for making their own imaginary pictures. There is a further and more subtle point. An artist may be most conscientious in getting all the individual details of costume, furniture, etc. correct, and yet, in creating his scene, in the stance, gestures, facial expression of his figures, he is giving his own, often subtly anachronistic, interpretation. No one knows how King John looked as he faced his barons at Runnymede, yet we have seen many pictures of a scowling John and a pictorial impression makes an even more powerful impact than a fanciful word-description. Some illustrators for educational publishers do not even do their home-work properly: I recently saw an Anglo-Saxon feast depicted in which the feasters used forks! Drawing your own picture is an entirely different case, for you know you are imagining the scene as you think it might have been. I think there are only two exceptions to the rule of no made-up pictures: first, a reconstruction from evidence of what, for instance, a Roman villa or a medieval village might have been like with an explanation in the text of what has been done and why; secondly, a famous artist's picture of a complete scene which can be studied critically as a work of art and examined for its accuracy against contemporary evidence. Notice that, in the reconstruction type, there need be no 'scene' involving human actions and emotions, while the work of art is specifically studied as a product of the imagination. Thus a reconstruction of a house at Pompeii is one thing, a scene of people fleeing in terror from Vesuvius, as represented in one famous picture, is another. The crucial point is that any illustrations of the second type must be clearly labelled as 'what the artist thought it might have looked like'. It is an interesting point that a picture can be unique and much admired as a work of art and yet historically inaccurate, and therefore apt to be misleading. Where this problem arises, it offers a good opportunity to discuss why it is a good picture but an untrustworthy source. There is a good discussion of two differing artists' impressions of the 'Death of Wolfe' in the Then and There book *The Struggle for Canada* by Barry Williams.

But the really troubling problem of pictures today is how to avoid capitulating to vulgarisation. It must be said that many of the history pictures produced for schools today – especially the coloured wall-pictures – are crude, vulgar and bad. Many teachers understandably feel they must use these because they have to compete with colour television, comics and so forth. Here is the old problem of how to help children develop a perceptive taste without imposing alien standards on them. Probably the best way is by encouraging criticism, on historical and artistic grounds, of pictures we think 'good' and 'bad', while comparing them with contemporary source pictures. Short of expensively accurate colour reproductions, black and white is nearly always the better medium, producing a more elegant line and often a more economically dramatic effect. The black and white pictures which graced children's books of the eighteenth century often make an immediate and satisfying impact.

With documents we meet a dilemma. The historian's concept of a source implies that we should present it entire and pure, or with dots scrupulously marking any omissions. But some of the documents we want to use for their intrinsic value and immediacy are too long and too intricate in sentence structure to be digested neat. Although we may pick them for vividness of phrase in some parts, the same texts may also be studded with abstract terms. In my judgement we should not lay them aside until they can be read in their entirety but adjust our historical consciences to make suitable modified versions. Of course this applies only to original sources which, at a particular stage, we deem to be enjoyable because well within the imaginative grasp of the group or individual; for many other fine pieces we must indeed wait till a later stage. But first, lest the piece remain a puzzling dead thing called a 'document', we have to set the scene in which it was actually written by an actual person. The clerk of a medieval manor court furiously scribbled in his abbreviated Latin this catalogue of misdeeds. This log of sea-exploration was penned by a sailor in a rolling ship's cabin by the light of a ship's lantern, and this one when marooned in an Arctic hut where the ink froze. If a seventeenth-century will is to be used for social history we must reconstruct the possible scene when the old man was making his last will and testament. Sometimes we have a magnificent description of the actual circumstances, as in the case of Captain Scott's last writings – moving words which all the young should meet at some stage. The point about proper preparation can also apply sometimes to visual material. The faded sepia photographs taken by Birdie Bowers on that last journey of Scott's do not make their full impact until the viewers have been brought to realise the incredible difficulties of photography in such circumstances and the marvel that we have this record at all.

As for the actual text, I believe we should have no compunction in cutting out unnecessary verbiage in order to make the vivid phrases stand out, sometimes combining original text with précis in brackets and sometimes supplying a paraphrase for a difficult sentence by placing after it (he means . . .). Sometimes it is the sheer amount of detail which must be thinned out, as, for instance, in the descriptions of Tudor coronation processions or Queen Elizabeth I's progresses, where the vivid detail gives a rich feast for the imagination but there is just too much of it. Again, a will begins with much tedious formula which can be summarised in order to get on to the real heart of it in the bequests which tell so much about social life. In all such editing our aim is to keep the authentic text where its phrases are sharp and telling and to adapt without distortion. We can call our versions adaptations and so salve our consciences. In addition, the actual physical form of some documents can itself be fascinating: the long pipe-roll, the tally-stick receipt, the charter hung with a fringe of seals, the apprentice indenture cut in half by a wavy line. It is fun to make facsimiles of these: I have heard of a boy whose weekend was dedicated with utter absorption to 'making' an Anglo-Saxon writ.

Work-cards are becoming increasingly popular as a way of presenting source material for individual or group research. A 'work-card' (to be distinguished from a work-sheet) should isolate a manageable item from an original document and/or an authentic contemporary illustration, together, probably, with some explanation and some glossary definitions, and possibly suggestions for what to do with the material, though these may be quite unnecessary. The essential component is therefore an intriguing statement (whether in word or picture) which comes up out of the past to hit you because it offers strange new information or poses an interesting problem. This is the antithesis of an undistinguished series of sentences giving general information from a secondary source: it is the difference between a newly-minted coin and an old worn one. Items can progress in difficulty as they will also in length, until the student passes beyond the need for short extracts ready isolated for him. But whatever the level, within the range of schooling up to about sixteen I believe we must exercise the kind of editorial handling I have been describing.

Analysis proceeds from curiosity shooting its questions like arrows into the sources, or taking a knife to dissect information, to the next stage of assembling and sorting what has been discovered. Don't let us minimise the importance of this, even for young children. One of the glories of the human animal is that he can bring together discrete items of information, to arrange, categorise, name and make patterns with them. The development of this faculty begins where exploration begins, but in the classroom there is a danger that it gets restricted because so much material has been pre-sorted in books and perhaps also in teacher's notes. So, although it slows up the process of learning, we need to take particular care in helping the young to sort information into categories for themselves, to find their own headings and work out their own arrangements in pattern or sequence. Every exercise in rational arrangement is an exercise in logic (though artistic arrangement may be governed by different laws), and we must give full weight to the educational value of this stage in understanding. To give a few obvious examples, prehistoric and medieval artefacts can be classified according to use and period, the abundant material on Elizabethan life can be arranged under headings such as dress, homes, towns, work, leisure and so on, inventions in the Industrial Revolution can be arranged in a cause-and-effect pattern, an evolutionary sequence can be worked out for, say, ships. The justification for such work (over and above training in logical arrangement) lies in the power which it gives the young researcher over his material, so that, out of the pieces, he can create for himself a 'whole' such as we will consider a little later.

Remembering the Adam myth, naming does appear to be a peculiar delight and prerogative of the human species and certainly children share delight in mastering the proper technical names for the things they have been analysing and categorising. This is the point behind the analytical drawing of, say, the parts of a castle or a monastery, or a suit of armour, or a steam engine. Here labelling accurately is a proper intellectual exercise, giving the joy of mastery. Names go with making patterns: in studying exploration, places and routes have to be plotted on a map; the 'rise and fall' of Napoleon can equally be plotted on a graph by the sequence of battles and treaties. The vital point here is that the young should, wherever possible, translate the information gathered from books into their own map or diagram, rather than copying a ready-made one from the book. We are sometimes guilty of doing too much, and the principle I am urging here is that we should give material to the young in as nearly 'raw' a state as we think they can take in order that they may do something with it for themselves.

But at a more advanced level of political and economic history there is a real problem. Writers and teachers probably see their task as that of reducing very complex and detailed raw material to order and pattern. Where the mass of information is so unwieldy it surely must be shaped into a structure beforehand. What can the secondary-stage boy or girl do with this ready-made material but take it over and learn it off? Increasingly, of course, there are perceptive writers who try to leave little spaces for individual thought and initiative, but in the main the average secondary text-book does all the analysis, imposes all the patterns and settles all the questions of motive or cause and effect. So we get 'three causes of the French Revolution', 'four stages in Parliamentary Reform' or 'five causes of the First World War'. It is only too easy to copy and learn these and reproduce them at O level. In reaction against 'copying the book', I have met American students who have been taught that, since the great crime is plagiarism, they should write down nothing but their own 'creative ideas'. This – to put it mildly – hardly works in history. There must be a mean between two extremes. History books have to be used for their information without reproducing their exact patterns or arrangements. Perhaps there are three methods which in combination can help us to resolve this dilemma. The first is that writers of school text-books should deliberately aim at setting out material which leads to the posing of a question rather than the giving of a definitive answer. The second is the well-used method of setting written work in the form of problems or questions to which the answer is not directly given in the book. The third is the method of setting problems on actual documents to which the text-book supplies the necessary background of information but the exercise is one of deducing something from the text itself. These are obviously not new methods, but the point still needs to be made. It is also possible sometimes to take a conventional subject from an unconventional angle, as, for instance, the mid-eighteenth-century political scene in Europe, seen, not from the point of view of 'the causes of the Seven Years' War', but from that of Boswell, the inquisitive traveller and eager cultivator of celebrities, or the Peninsular War from the angle of experiences in Wellington's army.

Analysis is for the service of wholeness in understanding – a good servant but a bad master. Collecting and sorting information is for a purpose, either an individual or a group one, an objective which will express our own imaginative response to the whole topic and which we can communicate to others. So we discuss in the group: what shall we *do* about it? And since, if we have found out something we enjoy, we generally want to tell someone else, an intermediate stage towards the main objective can be that of giving individual talks to the rest of the group on our own particular finds. Thus different aspects are gathered together and wholeness begins to emerge. Understanding in wholeness is ultimately the response of the whole personality, with imagination and feeling as well as intellect. It has been one of our great discoveries in the last half century or so that such an educational experience is to be attained through the pursuit of large imaginative objectives rather than little piece-meal lessons. So we are all familiar now with the main forms these objectives take: the mounting of an exhibition for the rest of the school, the writing and production of plays or television programmes, artistic response through imaginative pictures, or through mime, dance or music, the creation of a book or newspaper, puppets or figures in costume. It is, perhaps, worth reflecting a little on the educational values which come together in these activities. All of them contain in varying proportions ingredients of practice in fundamental skills mingled with imaginative interpretation and artistic creation in different media. Take the exhibition idea, for instance. At first sight it is the skills aspect that meets the eye. Here is splendid opportunity for categorising and arranging; the manual skills come into play in modelling exhibits etc., literary skills in presenting information in wall-sheets and clear descriptive labels, but the background must be created in imaginative painting or in reconstructions. If a guide-book to the exhibition is prepared or talks given on it, the group must have an over-all picture of what the times were like in which the people of the exhibition lived. Some work for exhibitions can reach a really creative standard. I remember a beautiful set of medieval Months of the Year adapted from manuscript illuminations and carried out in appliqué needlework and collage. Beautiful lettering and decoration executed with loving care can go to the production of a medieval book in which free drawing catches the spirit of the times; equally figures to illustrate costume can be works of art.

Making your own book is now a common activity in most schools, but it can be none the less wonderful – to the boy or girl who creates and decorates it, adding the distinctive cover which is the special mark of authorship, and, I think, also to the teacher who reflects on all it symbolises in terms of the human impulse to communicate what interests, in the language of word and picture. Even college students are not too sophisticated to become involved in such a project. I have observed that quite often they find a long essay the most satisfying part of their course and enjoy dressing up their work very beautifully, even to illustrations and fancy cover. Returning to school productions, if we analyse the literary element in them, I think at both primary and secondary level we can encourage three types of writing: informative, argumentative and imaginative. Each has its own value as a training in handling words, but I see them in a rising scale of achievement in the sense that imaginative writing involves feeling and sensitivity to a human situation which go beyond even argument. The argumentative can be great fun, bringing out a sharp wit sometimes. I have in mind, for instance a dialogue between an enclosing landlord and a peasant farmer, an American revolutionary and a loyalist, a French aristocrat and one of the Paris mob. Speeches are also a vehicle for argument, so is an imaginary newspaper which focuses on such a thorny topic as the abolition of the Corn Laws or the case against slavery. But the imaginative interpretation of historical experience is ultimately the most personal. How many touching or eloquent or vividly intimate tones we meet in those imaginary diaries, letters or eye-witness descriptions of battle or riot! Junior school children, seeing the Battle of Hastings through the eyes of a Saxon or Norman wife, could mingle their sense of the 'otherness' of the battle with very present-day experience of family partings and waitings. A middle-school girl writing a letter home with great relish about the hard discipline endured as one of Cromwell's soldiers, adds: 'P.S. Of course God is on our side.' With equal relish medieval villagers duck a scold: 'A proper scold she be. 'Twas like living next door to a hurricane when she go on at her husband.' An authentic letter home from early colonists asking for useful men and supplies evoked a sharp imaginary reply about the cost and the difficulties of transport. 'Additions' to Mr. Pepys' diary describing the Plague and Fire caught something of his style quite spontaneously.

One particularly stimulating type of book to make is what I would call a 'Then and Now' book, that is, a book of contrasts. The theme may be social life in a certain age, or, more specifically, farming methods and machines, kitchens and cooking, clothes, transport, or a dozen other possibilities. The method requires a good sorting process of the period material, and then the collecting and arranging of modern parallels or contrasts. For the historical side, pictures can be collected from various sources; for the modern equivalents, picture magazines, advertisements, catalogues, brochures etc. generally supply material in plenty. Inventing and writing the captions and explanations exercises verbal skills, and much discussion grows out of the comparisons. Take, for instance, the age-old farming work of ploughing and harrowing with oxen or horses and reaping by hand with sickle or scythe: what a change, when the farm worker now sits on a tractor and a combine-harvester presents bags of grain ready threshed from the field! Or the modern kitchen: children take the hot and cold water taps, the fridge, the electric stove, mixer and washing-machine for granted, until they look at pictures of medieval women cooking food in a pot over a fire or washing by the stream. Even abstract themes can be treated in such a book of contrasts, with both text and pictures. For instance, the eighteenth-century unreformed Parliament can be illustrated by many vivid pictures while newspapers and magazines of today supply the contrasts.

'Standing in other people's shoes' means, above all, for the young, some form of drama, mime or movement in which they respond imaginatively in their own persons. We recognise this educationally in the universal presence of dramatic activity in school, from the free acting of the children who played at Joseph and his brethren to the developed drama of a scene which features an imaginary meeting between Elizabeth I and Mary, Queen of Scots. It is a Protean activity with many shapes. I remember a primary school group who spent several weeks in Viking adventures. They built the dragon prow of a ship and made themselves helmets, shields and weapons. When acting their adventures overseas, they simply sat on the floor in line behind their dragon head and rowed away with gusto. One story of rowing through a storm told how the leader sang to the wind. This evoked an unprepared response from a West Indian child: swinging backwards and forwards as she rowed, she began to sing, composing words and music together in the rhythm. Miming scenes from Drake's voyage round the world sprang into life for twelve-year-olds who found his swoops on to the Pacific coast of South America very much to their liking. A shore-exploring party comes on a lad asleep in charge of a mule-train laden with gold: 'We took the gold and left the lad' – what glee went into that miming! Like the traditional puppet contests of Crusader and Muslim in Palermo, I have seen Beowulf fighting a terrific puppet battle with Grendel, and Gawain facing the

Green Knight. The St. Francis play I mentioned moved a stage further on, with dialogue that was finally worked out in writing, and this raises the question of how freely boys and girls at the secondary level will continue to express historical experience dramatically. Do they still enjoy imagining themselves in other people's shoes to the extent of writing or acting a rôle? Probably they do during the first two years beyond the primary stage. It is not so much that fantasy fades after that, but that it is focused more closely on 'myself, my identity and my possible futures'. Obviously there will be great variation and one plays this game by ear. I am told by one teacher in a comprehensive school that the students go on enjoying imaginative writing and acting better than any other form of historical activity, but it is hopeless to force an activity of this kind when the spark is not kindled.

Finally, visual form and colour stand in their own right as means through which the past can be re-created. This often means translating authentic verbal description into this new medium through the inward eye which can envision, for instance, the fabulous palace of the Kublai Khan with its red and green dragons, as revealed to the amazed gaze of Marco Polo, or the richness of Queen Elizabeth I going to chapel under the eager eyes of Paul Hentzner, or the great sea monster 'with much demonstration of teeth' that chilled the souls of Sir Humphrey Gilbert's sailors. Sometimes the artistic impulse is to translate from one art form into another, as when figures from a medieval manuscript such as the Luttrell Psalter become subjects for lino-cuts. Sometimes the whole visual response to a topic can be drawn together in a frieze of original pictures expressed in the style of the period, as in the case of Egyptian wall-painting or Greek vase painting. Always there will be a fruitful tension between the demands of historical accuracy and the play of creative inspiration, so that the picture can catch the spirit of the past and yet contain something of yourself.

In the later stages of school spontaneity perhaps flags and responses grow more complex. Moreover, those who are now emerging as potential artists and actors seek more sophisticated outlets. In creating pictures they are growing aware of perspective difficulties and the complications of figure and face drawing. Acting is no longer improvising a role, but studying a part in a play. The 'play way' is over. The imaginative element is, however, still vital in understanding history. Thus writing and producing drama for the stage or for television or for a film scenario remain important activities. There are also many modern historical plays to act. Here there is a critical as well as a creative activity, for some need to be scrutinised by the acting group for historical accuracy. Anouilh, in his

Thomas Becket, for instance, openly flouts history by making Becket's mother an Anglo-Saxon woman; here is matter for considerable argument on how allowable it is for a playwright or film-maker to change history to suit his own artistic purpose. But here we are slipping back into a critical, analytical approach to history. Very important– yes, but at the higher levels of 'O' and 'A', college and university work, the great problem becomes whether history perforce develops into a wholly analytical, critical study. High drama has not disappeared, but the pressures are on to cut it down to the size of our notebooks, and to substitute for people 'in the round' the more easily manipulated two-dimensional figures of the analytical text-books. I once suggested to some students that, instead of an essay on the causes of the downfall of Charles the Bold of Burgundy, they should write a scenario for a play or opera on the tragedy of Shakespearian proportions which was his life. No one did: by that time, perhaps, they were too imbued with the necessity of treating every subject analytically. Yet some emerge from this educational process still able to combine acute scholarship with high imaginative perception. They become the great historians. More ordinary mortals, like ourselves and many of our students, need, perhaps, more help in learning to enjoy history by re-creating it for ourselves.

7
And so to examinations

Has all this overflowing historical experience simply to be decanted at the end into the row of pint pots which are the examination papers to be written before school is finished with? Of course it is nonsense to suppose that the only purpose and result of one's experience of history is to write thirty- or forty-five-minute answers to other people's questions: growth in wisdom is not thus to be tested. But those pint pots at the end of the road are very real and they have to be filled just so – neither too much nor too little. It is worth remembering, incidentally, that examinations began in the medieval university as tests of would-be teachers rather than of students as such, in the sense that the licence to teach depended on surmounting hurdles of oral disputation. So today an examination can promote a useful gathering together of forces for the purpose of jumping the hurdle that leads to the next career-stage. The discipline of preparing for it, the organising of what you know, the demand for concentrated attention, not when you feel like it, but over just that particular span of time – these are salutary, if sometimes unpleasant, experiences. Examinations have their point.

But preparing for and writing standard examination papers has little to do with the growth of imaginative experience and the gradual understanding of what human living has been in the past and is today and should be tomorrow. Examination requirements impose two limitations. In the first place, it has been customary and convenient to set many history examination syllabuses in terms of a period of time to be covered fairly evenly, with attention to all the main events within it. But a 'period of history' is an adult concept (sometimes a very artificial one), whereas the young, I have suggested, envisage the past more easily in terms of a particular group of actors against their own background, or, alternatively, as one theme pursued through a time-span discarding other things happening alongside. 'Covering the set period' often precludes investigation in depth and is seldom compatible with pursuing themes. Secondly, in method, there is great pressure on the conscientious teacher to do too much by way of pre-digesting and patterning information beforehand because otherwise the class will not get on quickly enough. Thus, however well set, by its very nature the orthodox examination paper constricts the experience of history in several ways: it cuts the seamless robe up into little question-bits; the form of the questions puts the emphasis almost wholly on an analytical approach to knowledge ('give so many reasons or causes for this or that'); the limit on time forces answers into the cliché statement or dehydrated formulae that murder real history.

There is a further problem in respect of public examinations in particular: to achieve fairness in mass marking pattern answers have to be worked out, with marks allocated to each point. The temptation then is to prepare by learning pattern answers, while the examinee who treats the question in an individual way, but does not cover all the points, suffers. Many efforts have been made by examining boards to escape from this dilemma, but so long as the test takes the shape of the standard question paper the dilemma remains: either you must devise questions on the safe pattern–answer principle, or, if you venture to give opportunity for individual judgement or opinion, you must brave the slippery slopes of qualitative marking. The first is certainly safer. Thus, in general, examinations of the orthodox type, though socially and personally useful, do not measure real historical understanding nor provide a fitting finale to an experience of history which has found its expression in some creation like a play or a book.

There are, however, various ways of bridging the gap between 'real' history and examination history. The most complete is to put up and get accepted one's own examination syllabus for the CSE or 'O' level. This syllabus can be composed from themes such as I have suggested (or others, of course) which can be studied in depth and in the round, and only packaged up for tidy examination answers towards the end of the course. If individual project work within the syllabus can be presented for the examination as well, there is so much more opportunity for the full experience of history which is our real concern.

Secondly, examination boards and the teachers on them can make as much use as possible of the type of history paper which tests powers of reasoning and deduction, that is, method in handling evidence, rather than information. There has been an enlightened and welcome development here of papers setting exercises on given documents, in which the answers have to be deduced from what is given, or comparisons made between two different accounts of the same event, or similar exercises worked out. This seems to me to be a proper way in which to use the examination technique to test history. What it can discover is, not what facility the candidate has in serving up hard little nuggets of fact, but how far he or she has learnt to handle sources as a researcher looking for truth and using a variety of techniques in the search. It remains true that this kind of paper only tests one side of history study, the analytical, but the other side, the imaginative, remains stubbornly remote from examination techniques. It is possible, and not unknown, to ask candidates to write poems, musical compositions, or pieces of imaginative history work in a three-hour examination, but for many candidates the invitation to do so is hardly felicitous.

The third possibility is to put examinations firmly in their place, that is, not very high in the order of priorities. All the practical pressures to do well in them make it difficult not to let examinations occupy the centre of the stage. But, just as lower down in school children can learn tables and dates, but find their really absorbing experiences in quite another dimension, so the techniques of packaging up information for memorising accurately and for snipping out and presenting exactly the detail required by a question can be taught and practised as useful skills which do not spoil the real foci of interest. And they are useful skills. It is valuable both for teachers and students that the latter should be able to measure their achievement in such skills as accurate memorising and clarity of presentation by the fairly objective tests which examinations impose. For this purpose such tests are useful all the way up the secondary school, with the very important provisos that they do not loom up too often (perhaps only once a year), that they can be taken in one's stride and that in evaluating achievement they do not count for too much. One can make a useful analogy here with what goes on in the PE lesson. Disciplined precise drill in the coordination of muscles and limbs does not spoil the creativity of free movement and dance, rather it enhances the controlled spontaneity of artistic response.

In short, examination work need not damage the real study of history if we have our priorities right and see clearly the limitations of even the best examinations in what they can demand of the student and what the results can tell us about him–her. They cannot test the widening and deepening of human understanding as the young enter into the experience of history, they cannot really test their growing perceptions of right and wrong, justice and injustice, they cannot test the emotions of admiration, exhilaration, awe, horror, compassion, which are valid responses to the grandeurs and tragedies of history. As long as the study of history can nourish all these things, examinations remain useful servants, not masters.

8
Planning syllabuses:
some suggestions

This chapter is presented with full apologies to those teachers who have been working on these lines for a long time, to those who have newer and better ideas and to those who dislike other people's schemes anyway. It may, however, be useful to some if I put examples scattered throughout the book into some kind of loose order. I say 'loose', because I do not want to present 'tight' schemes for precise age-groups. History is pre-eminently a socialising study which can be carried on cooperatively in mixed age or ability groups and, since themes shade from the simpler to the more sophisticated, there are few clear dividing lines: topics can be adjusted to an earlier or a later stage, so that those missed earlier can be taken later. Editing history books for schools and finding that a single book is being profitably used in different ways by a surprisingly wide band of readers has convinced me that a rigid schematic organisation of material is not only unnecessary but inimical to a proper flexibility. Of course an orderly progression, year by year, through the centuries gives the chronological framework which may for some be the most desirable objective. But, as I have already argued, genuine experiences of understanding history are more important than carrying a string of 'memorable' events. To keep the order right – that Greeks come before Romans, or the English Revolution before the French – a class time-chart can be instituted from a fairly early stage and carried on from year to year, getting more sophisticated as it goes. Order is more important than date-line in the early stages when the passage of time measured out accurately in metres means little. It is the sequence that matters, so that words and pictures sprawling beyond their proper bounds in a primary school chart need not, in my view, cause undue anxiety.

I shall take, then, a broad division between junior and secondary stages and, within these, between the lower and the upper ends. The principle of selection, following my earlier arguments, is that of providing an appropriate range of historical experiences at each stage, rather than covering a certain amount of ground. At every stage, therefore, I should want the young to be discovering something about their historic selves and to enjoy some adventures in being other people. Both these types of experience are most satisfyingly realised in 'patches'. There is also the experience of change – 'progress', to use a rather ambiguous word – in history, which suggests threads of development to be traced through time. These not only show men discovering, inventing, changing ideas through the ages, but they can illuminate ideas of time and chronological order. So I suggest that Patches and Threads should form the pattern of our syllabus-making. The time allowed for each topic will naturally vary with individual teachers and circumstances, but if, say, three to four weeks were allowed for each, six or eight topics could be selected for the year, including one 'threads' topic which might appropriately come at the end. Indeed, the selection might move through my 1, 2, 3, categories below, in that order. A kind of spiral effect may be noticed, since something missed or taken more simply at an earlier stage can come round again for more advanced treatment.

These schemes can be called a 'history syllabus' in the sense that the core of each topic is a historical experience, but it need not be pursued in a unit time-tabled 'history lesson'. As I have said, history claims a wide *imperium* and a wide service in its use of other 'subjects'. So all these topics should be at home in integrated or combined studies programmes. Equally, although they are here presented with class groups in mind, all would lend themselves to pursuit by separate sub-groups, or by individuals doing independent project-work. When a whole group tackles a topic together, there are nearly always within it more specialised aspects which can be investigated separately. So I have sometimes suggested individual assignments, the results of which could be communicated to the whole group in talks. It follows, from the range of subjects and skills which can be drawn in, that teaching in partnerships or teams can be very fruitful, but, in so far as the central experience is historical, the 'historian's craft' is also central.

I have described each topic briefly, not attempting to give adequate coverage on the information involved, but in order to indicate motifs and special interests appropriate for this stage. Under 'activities' I have suggested various kinds of things to do appropriate to the topic. But all activity starts from exploration for oneself, so the initial activities of acquiring information from pictures and books and observations are common to all, although ranging in difficulty from the early use of pictures or street observations to the advanced reading of a document. Equally, the second stage of sorting what has been gleaned, recording it and preparing it for communication to others is also common to all, though carried out at very different levels. Language work in learning and using new words, often technical terms, and in many types of writing also goes on all the time. So, having drawn attention to these basic and important activities, I shall omit them in my particular suggestions. Finally, where possible, I have given a very simple book list, intended mainly for class-room research, but sometimes for the teacher's use.

1 Lower end of the junior school (ages about 8–10)

1.1 Topics about ourselves

1.1.1 *How our village/town/locality/housing estate grew*
Units will vary according to locality but they have to be of manageable size and immediacy in terms of the imagination and, where possible, walkable. The children can focus on a study of streets, houses, shops, churches, clubs, etc. and the human needs they meet, when they were made or built, and how. The aim is to see the locality, not in terms of tarmac, bricks and stones, but as a place shaped by people and their needs, growing as more people come. This is essentially a neighbourhood topic, and some neighbourhoods may present problems which make them unsuitable.

ACTIVITIES
Communicating information verbally
Collecting and discussing inscriptions and dates on buildings, monuments, pillar-boxes and so on
Listing community needs and how they have been met in the shops, in supplies of water, gas, electricity and so on
Making simple maps and plans to show how the community grew
Making a model to show the pattern of the community
Making a picture record

BOOKS
For the pupil
Most material will be local but see also:
Bowood, R., *The Story of Houses and Homes*, Ladybird.
Gregory, B., *Homes, Roads, Railways, Canals*, Read All About It, Wheaton.
Rowland, K., *The Shape of Towns*, Looking and Seeing, Ginn.
Sauvain, P., *Maps and How to Read Them*, Franklin Watts.
Thompson, S., *Shops and Markets*, Fact Finders, Macdonald.
Vialls, C., *Cast-Iron, Windmills and Watermills, Crossing the River, Roads*, Industrial Archaeology Series, Black.

Vince, C., *History All Around You*, Wheaton of Exeter.
Voysey, A., *Looking at the Countryside*, Local Search, Routledge & Kegan Paul.
Bridges and Tunnels, Ports and Harbours, Macdonald First Library, Macdonald.
Trains, Roads, Homes, Post, Farms, Macdonald Starters, Macdonald.

For the teacher
Douch, R., *Local History and the Teacher*, Routledge & Kegan Paul.
Ferguson, I. S. and Simpson, E. J., *Teaching Local History*, Moray House Publications.
Richardson, J., *The Local Historian's Encyclopedia*, Historical Publications Ltd.

AUDIO-VISUAL MATERIAL
Village sites, Slide Centre. 12 colour slides with notes.
Development of towns, Slide Centre. 12 Colour slides with notes.

1.1.2 *What our fathers and mothers/grandparents/great-grandparents did when they were children*
This amounts to family life 30, 50, 70 or 100 years ago. It starts from stories and objects which children collect in their families and bring to school. Material – from old post cards, photographs, magazines, as well as reminiscences – can be arranged under headings like houses, food, clothes, play and school. It can then be discussed from the viewpoint of comparisons between Then and Now.

ACTIVITIES
Making large wall-sheets of information in pictures and writing
Tape-recording reminiscences of older generations (which involves working out the right questions beforehand and assembling the information afterwards)
Arranging a museum corner in the room, with labels for the exhibits
Making a Then and Now book
Dramatising scenes from the life of boys and girls at a given time
Writing stories about their lives and adventures

BOOKS FOR THE PUPIL
Delgado, A., *Edwardian England*, Then and There, Longman.
Harris, N., *The Thirties, The Forties and Fifties*, Macdonald.
Hoare, H., (ed. Unstead) *World War Two, Turn of the Century*, Macdonald.
Hughes, J., *A Victorian Sunday*, Wayland Eyewitness Books, Wayland.

Kelsall, F., *How We Used to Live 1908–1918, –1925, –1945, –in Victorian Times,* Macdonald/Yorkshire Television.

Speed, P. F., *Learning and Teaching in Victorian Times,* Then and There, Longman.

Stuart, D., *A Child's Day Through the Ages,* Harrap.

Taylor, B., *Picture Reference Book of the Victorians,* Brockhampton Press.

Trease, G., *Britain Yesterday,* Blackwell.

Unstead, R. J., *The Twenties,* Macdonald.

Wood, R., *Children 1773–1890,* History at Source, Evans.

AUDIO-VISUAL MATERIAL

Early this century, BBC Radiovision. Colour filmstrip with notes to accompany radio broadcast in 'History not so long ago' series.

Elizabeth: 25 years a queen, Ivan Berg. Cassette.

Fifty years of royal broadcasts 1924-74, BBC. Cassette.

George VI, Rank Film Library. Colour filmstrip with notes.

Homefront, BBC Radiovision. Colour filmstrip with notes to accompany radio broadcast in 'History not so long ago' series.

Life in Edwardian England, folio 3: Health, food and holidays; life in the country; childhood; youth and education. Slide Centre. 12 colour slides with notes (notes need simplifying).

The Queen's Silver Jubilee (1977), Woodmansterne. 18 colour slides with notes.

See also the audio-visual material suggested under 1.3.2. Although most of the material on the two world wars for the 13-16 year-olds is too difficult, some of the slides, pictures and facsimiles could be used.

1.2 Topics about different people

1.2.1 *The first people (prehistoric men)*

This blanket title covers many thousand years and evolving cultures, but for the first introduction to how early people lived it is best to fix on one stage – perhaps the Neolithic – and develop a picture in the round. Later, the evolution of skills through the Bronze and Iron Ages can be tackled. Here, at the outset, the emphasis will be on families working hard to get their livelihood, making tools and homes out of what they could find, seeking their food, having hunting adventures, facing danger. The probable climate, surroundings and types of animal will be important. Inventiveness and improvisation in simple things (e.g. putting a handle on a tool, setting traps, making bows and arrows) will be a key-note. If the school is near a prehistoric site, this becomes a focal point and may shape the topic. Essentially this is a topic for imaginative reconstruction and play.

ACTIVITIES

Recording in pictures and writing, on wall-sheets or charts, information gathered about clothes, food, homes, tools

Playing at the various occupations, the play perhaps developing into more connected dramatic scenes

Doing language work in new words connected with early men

Constructing a model home and equipment

Making tools and weapons for acting

Telling and writing adventure stories

Painting imaginary scenes

Making models of prehistoric animals with labels

BOOKS FOR THE PUPIL

Hadenius, S., and Jannip, B., *How They Lived in the Stone Age, How They Lived in the Bronze Age,* Lutterworth Press.

Hume, E. G., *Days Before History,* The Pilgrim Way, book 1, Blackie.

Neurath, M., and Turner, M., *They Lived Like This in the Old Stone Age,* Macdonald.

Osborn, J. R., *Stone Age to Iron Age,* Focus on History, Longman.

Place, R., *Prehistoric Britain,* Then and There, Longman.

Sauvain, P., *Prehistoric Britain,* Imagining the Past, Macdonald.

Thompson, S., *Early Man,* Fact Finders, Macmillan.

Prehistoric Life, Macdonald Visual Books, Easy Reading Edition, Macdonald.

Stone Age Man, Buried History, The First Farmers, Macdonald Starters, Macdonald.

AUDIO-VISUAL MATERIAL

Cavemen and hunters, M. Neurath, Longman/Common Ground. Colour filmstrip with notes.

Farmers and craftsmen, M. Neurath, Longman/Common Ground. Colour filmstrip with notes.

Stonehenge, Slide Centre. 2 sets of slides with notes.

1.2.2 *Joseph and his brethren: an ancient Egyptian topic*

If ancient Egyptian civilisation is to be introduced at an early stage – and it can make a great appeal – the story of Joseph makes a good lead-in, without worrying about problems of literal historicity or chronology. The story branches out into the strange and exciting land of Egypt, its climate, the importance of the Nile, the people, the Pharoahs. In detail, their clothes and homes, the making of paper and the invention of hieroglyphics, their gods and beliefs about the after-life, burial customs, pyramids and temples – all provide rich material for the imagination and can be studied directly from pictures and objects.

ACTIVITIES
Reading aloud parts of Joseph's story from the Bible
Giving talks to the group on, e.g., the flooding of the Nile, papyrus
    grass to paper, Egyptian gods, the Cat and the Beetle in Egypt,
    building a pyramid
Copying hieroglyphics and putting your own name into them
Making models of Egyptian monuments
Making a class-room frieze of Egyptian scenes in their style (e.g. a
    feast, boats on the Nile, bringing a tribute to Pharoah
Making small figures or puppets in Egyptian dress (using pleated
    white paper for linen)
Dramatising or miming the story of Joseph

BOOKS
For the pupil
Breasted, J., *Ancient Times*, Ginn.
Davies, P., and Stewart, P., *Tutankhamun's Egypt*, Wayland.
Sheppard, E. J., *Ancient Egypt*, Then and There, Longman.
Unstead, R. J., *See Inside an Egyptian Town*, Hutchinson.
Joseph and his Brothers, *The Pyramid Builders*, Macdonald Starters,
    Macdonald.

AUDIO-VISUAL MATERIAL
The Ancient World, E. J. Sheppard, Then and There, Longman. Set of 4
    filmstrips with notes.
Joseph, N. Makinson, Visual Publications. Colour filmstrip with
    notes.
Life in Ancient Egypt, M. Neurath, Longman/Common Ground.
    Colour filmstrip with notes.
The rise of Egyptian civilisation, Encyclopaedia Britannica. Colour
    filmstrip with notes.
The story of Joseph, L. Diamond, Ladybird. Colour filmstrip.

1.2.3 *Life of a Greek or Roman boy or girl*
Again, before the time comes for a fuller study of these great
civilisations, it is enjoyable to stand in the shoes of a boy or girl – boy is
easier because there is more information.

i. *Greek*   The best time and place is mid-fifth-century Athens, just
before the Peloponnesian War. An Athenian citizen's home, the
upbringing and life of children, boys at school (with the *paedogogus*, the
gymnasium, music, Athens (Acropolis, Agora, Pnyx, etc.), its
festivals, plays and games – on all this there is detailed and exciting
information with striking social contrasts with life today (political

contrasts can be left until later). The group can go back to the Trojan War, to Ulysses, to the Persian Wars, especially the battles of Marathon and Thermopylae, as stories children would hear.

ACTIVITIES
Giving talks on information gained from Greek vase-paintings
Making a model of Athens or the Acropolis
Doing language study on words we get from Greek (e.g. *paedogogus*)
Making a class-room frieze of Athenian scenes in the style of vase-painting
Writing stories, e.g. about a day at school, a visit to the gymnasium, the great yearly procession, the Olympic games
Acting some of the Homeric stories
Discussing whether you would rather live Then or Now

ii. *Roman*   Possible focal points are Rome at the time of Caesar's murder, a family living near Vesuvius at the time of the great eruption (A.D. 79), Roman Britain at the time of Hadrian (or according to the date of a local site). Pattern as for the Greek topic: houses and home life, schooling, games, background of Rome or other locality, amphitheatre shows, great events and stories from past Roman history. Pictorial material varies: inscriptions and sculpture (not exciting for beginners), mosaics and frescoes (more so), objects dug up (sandals, lamps, cosmetics, writing materials, etc.). Reconstructions of Roman villas catch the imagination more than archaeological remains. An interesting point is the difficulty of doing sums with Roman numerals, and why.

ACTIVITIES
Talks to the group, e.g. on Roman 'central heating' and baths, gladiatorial shows, construction of Roman roads, what a Roman town looked like, famous Roman buildings.
Learning Roman numerals and trying to calculate with them
Doing language study on words from Latin (e.g. *miles, lux*)
Telling or writing stories, e.g. the day Caesar was murdered, escape from Vesuvius, building Hadrian's Wall
Modelling a Roman hypocaust system, a villa, an aqueduct, and amphitheatre or forum
Painting pictures, e.g. of Vesuvius in eruption or making Roman pictures in some kind of mosaic
Dramatising exciting scenes
Discussing whether you would rather live Then or Now

BOOKS
For the pupil
Bentley, J. D., *The Ancient Olympic Games*, Hulton.
Crosher, J., *The Greeks*, Peoples of the Past, Macdonald.
Cruse, A., *The Book of Myths*, Harrap.
Kupfer, G. H., *Legends of Greece and Rome*, Harrap.
Liversidge, J., *Roman Britain*, Then and There, Longman.
Liversidge, J., *Roman Gaul*, Then and There, Longman.
Mozley, J., *The Wooden Horse of Troy*, Franklin Watts.
Purves, A., *Growing up in Ancient Greece*, Wayland.
Purves, A., *Growing up in Ancient Rome*, Wayland.
Sheppard, E. J., *Ancient Athens*, Then and There, Longman.
Sherwin-White, N., *Ancient Rome*, Then and There, Longman.
Stuart, D., *The Boy through the Ages*, Harrap.
Stuart, D., *The Girl through the Ages*, Harrap.
Unstead, R. J., *Living in Pompeii*, Black.
Unstead, R. J., *See Inside a Roman Town*, Hutchinson.
Ancient Greece, Greek Myths and Legends, Macdonald Junior Reference, Macdonald.
Ancient Rome, Macdonald Junior Reference, Macdonald.

For the teacher
Freeman, K., *Schools of Hellas*, Kennikat Press.
Quennell, M. and C. H. B., *Everyday Things in Greece*, Batsford.
Quennell, M. and C. H. B., *Everyday Things in Rome*, Batsford.

AUDIO-VISUAL MATERIAL
The Ancient World, E. J. Sheppard, Then and There, Longman/Common Ground. Set of 4 filmstrips with notes
Athens, Sparta, and *Persia*, M. Forrest, Cambridge University Press, for Schools Council.
The Parthenon, BBC Radiovision. Colour filmstrip with notes to accompany radio broadcast in 'World History' series.
The Tale of Troy, Visual Publications. Colour filmstrip with notes.
Life in Ancient Greece, C. A. Stott, Longman/Common Ground. Colour filmstrip with notes.
Life in the Roman Empire, C. A. Stott, Longman/Common Ground. Colour filmstrip with notes.

1.2.4 *Viking adventurers*
The central theme is the fiord-people who go adventuring in their boats, starting with their log-houses and life in the homeland,

building boats, reasons for sailing out, then adventures on the high
seas and returning to feast. Stories from the sagas can be used. At this
stage heroic stories are better than the story of Viking invasions of
England. There is rich background material on the decoration of
ships (see the great dragon prows), on the wonderful metal-work of
helmets, swords and shields, and – on the literary side – in the
Beowulf descriptions of the hall and ship-burial. Sutton Hoo evidence
of another kind of ship burial can be used. Stories of Norse gods and
heroes of Asgard make splendid heroic story-telling. The language of
runes and the origin of our days of the week can be introduced.

ACTIVITIES

Talks to the group on fiords, Viking homes, how Viking boats were
  built and how today we have rediscovered them, Viking gods, lands
  to which Vikings adventured
Constructing a Viking boat or modelling a dragon prow
Making and painting shields, swords, helmets
Making a frieze of Viking ships
Painting pictures, e.g. feasting in the hall, Beowulf's fight with
  Grendel, a ship burial
Writing adventure stories of exploring and raiding
Acting the Beowulf story or other stories from sagas or dramatising
  the stories with puppets
Learning Norwegian braid-weaving
Doing language study on words we get from Scandinavia
Making a set of pictures on the meanings of the days of the week

BOOKS

For the pupil
Boucher, A., *A Viking Raider*, People of the Past, Oxford.
Carter, A. M., *One Day With the Vikings*, Day Book, Tyndall.
Elgin, K., *The First Book of the Norse Legends*, Edmund Ward.
Gibson, M., *The Vikings*, Peoples of the Past, Macdonald.
Keary, A. and E., *The Heroes of Asgard*, Macmillan.
Onclincx, G., *Einar the Viking*, Black.
Proctor, G. *The Vikings*, Then and There, Longman.
Sutcliff, R., *Beowulf*, Bodley Head.
Sutcliff, R., *Heroes of Asgard*, translation from the sagas, Everyman
  (and other editions).
Wilmot-Buxton, E. M., *Told By the Northmen*, Harrap.
Vikings, Macdonald Starters, Macdonald.

For the teacher
Wilson, D., *The Vikings and their Origins*, Thames & Hudson.

AUDIO-VISUAL MATERIAL
The Vikings, Visual Publications. Colour filmstrip with notes.
Vikings at home and *Vikings abroad,* J. Simpson, Visual Publications. 2
   colour filmstrips with notes and cassette (need to simplify notes and
   possibly be selective in use of frames).

1.3   Threads to trace

These threads will probably pick up information already acquired
from patches and relate this to what went before or came after. The
emphasis is on curiosity, discovery, invention ingenuity, e.g. the
many ways in which men have solved practical problems of living.

1.3.1   *Ways of communicating by signals, signs, runes, writing*
Many children love secret sign languages and will eagerly invent their
own. The great question is *why* did early peoples invent signs and
writing (for practical purposes? to give religious power?). Start with
the signal and sign systems of primitive peoples (using smoke, knots,
twigs, signs on trees, etc.). Then follow Egyptian writing and its
materials, Mesopotamian (cuneiform writing and clay tablets),
development of an alphabetic system and our alphabet from Greek.
'Cracking' unknown languages can be illustrated from the Rosetta
Stone. Other systems of writing in the world today (e.g. Chinese,
Arabic and Hebrew) can be compared with ours. The topic can be
extended to modern ways of sending messages quickly (postal
systems, telegraph, telephone, radio, 'Early Bird' and so on).

ACTIVITIES
Talks to the group on different sorts of signal or writing
Drawing up a glossary of technical words needed
Making an illustrated chart or book of signals, signs and types of
   writing, explaining where they come from
Mounting an exhibition for the school on 'Means of Communication',
   complete with posters, explanatory labels and a guide-book
Inventing a secret class language of your own

BOOKS FOR THE PUPIL
Bartlett, S., *Books, Pictures, Signs and Symbols,* Chatto, Boyd & Oliver.
Bear, J., *Communication,* Macdonald Visual Books, Macdonald.
Driscoll, V., *The Story of Books,* Toppers History, Macdonald.
Eldon, K. and M., *Tom-Tom to Television,* Wayland.
Goaman, M., *How Writing Began,* Faber.
Goodall, F. J., *The Story of Radio,* Ladybird.
Gregory, O. B., *Books and Writing,* Read All About It, Wheaton.

Knight, B., *Sending Messages*, Blackwell.
Metcalfe, L., *The Post Office and Its Services*, Blandford.
Page, R., *The Story of the Post*, Black.
Priestly, A. E., *Heraldry*, Ladybird.
Siddle, W. D., *The Story of Newspapers*, Ladybird.
How Writing Began, Macdonald Starters, Macdonald.

AUDIO-VISUAL MATERIAL
Writing: origins and development, D. Wyllie. Colour filmstrip with notes.
Signs and signals, Slide Centre. 12 colour slides with notes.
History of the telephone instrument, Post Office. Wallchart.
The History of the Post Office, Slide Centre. 12 colour slides with notes.
Telegraph and telephone services and communication by satellite, Slide Centre.
    12 colour slides with notes.
The story of newspapers, W. D. Siddle, Ladybird. Colour filmstrip to
    accompany Ladybird book.

1.3.2 *Ways of travelling*
This can go right back to early man – how they got about, first boats,
the invention of the wheel – or can be a predominantly modern study
on steam locomotion, the internal combustion engine, flight and
space travel, or again focus on a particular topic, e.g. roads and
canals, bridges and tunnels, the evolution of the modern ship or
motor-car. There is much pictorial material and there is a good
opportunity to learn how to put it in logical sequence.

ACTIVITIES
Talks to the group showing how different means of locomotion
    worked
Drawing up a glossary of technical terms
Making an evolutionary chart or book with pictures and explanations
Making a set of models to illustrate stages of development and then
    mounting an exhibition
Finding out about some of the great inventors (Watt, Stephenson,
    Telford, Brunel, the Wright brothers and so on) and discussing
    what made them go on in the face of disappointments

BOOKS FOR THE PUPIL
Books dealing with this topic are innumerable – these are only a few:
Benson, R., *Ships*, Macdonald.
Bowood, R., *The Story of Flight*, Ladybird.
Bowood, R., *The Story of Railways*, Ladybird.
Bucknall, R., *Trains*, Macdonald.

Cameron, A. D., *Thomas Telford and the Transport Revolution*, Then and There, Longman.

Carey, D., *The Story of the Motor Car*, Ladybird.

Ellacott, S., *The Story of Aircraft*, Methuen.

Ellacott, S., *Wheels on the Road*, Methuen.

Ellacott, S., *The Story of Ships*, Methuen.

France, C., *Discovering Sailing Ships*, University of London Press.

Greenwood, M., *Roads and Canals in the Eighteenth Century*, Then and There, Longman.

Greenwood, M., *The Railway Revolution*, Then and There, Longman.

Hammersley, A. and Perry, G. A., *Railways and Rail Transport*, Blandford.

Lewenhak, S., *Steamships and Shipbuilders in the Industrial Revolution*, Then and There, Longman.

Munson, K., *Aircraft*, Macdonald.

Murphy, J. S., *How They Were Built: Bridges*, Oxford.

St John Thomas, D., *The Motor Revolution*, Then and There, Longman.

Unstead, R. J., *Travel by Road Through the Ages*, Black.

Wyatt, R., *Cars*, Macdonald.

Trains, Macdonald Starters, Macdonald.

AUDIO-VISUAL MATERIAL

Speed, London Transport. Wallchart.

Transport, Our World Wallcharts, no. 2, Macmillan.

Development of transport by air, Slide Centre. 16 colour slides with notes.

Development of transport on land, Slide Centre. 16 colour slides with notes.

Development of transport by water, Slide Centre. 16 colour slides with notes.

Roads and road transport, folios 1-3, Slide Centre. 3 sets of colour slides with notes.

Transport by sea and air, R. Colquhoun, Nicholas Hunter. 25 colour slides with notes.

Canals, folios 1 and 2, Slide Centre. 12 colour slides with notes.

The London underground railway, G. Perry, Slide Centre. 12 colour slides with notes.

The story of lighthouses, lightships and lifeboats, O. Reed, Ladybird. Colour filmstrip to accompany Ladybird book.

Seadogs and sailing ships, BBC Radiovision. Colour filmstrip and notes to accompany radio broadcast in 'History Long Ago' series.

Ballooning, BBC Radiovision. Colour filmstrip and notes to accompany radio broadcast in 'Exploration Earth' series.

The story of roads, Educational Productions. Colour filmstrip with notes.

Moon rocket, BBC Radiovision. Colour filmstrip with notes to accompany radio broadcast in 'Nature' series.

2 Upper end of the junior school (ages about 10–11+)

Topics not taken at the lower stage can be picked up and explored in greater detail. Some suggestions below are based on this assumption; some are new.

2.1 Topics about ourselves

2.1.1 *Our own town/locality*
The unit can now be bigger (the whole town or area), geographical factors can be more specifically studied and the history of the community explored in more detail. Place and street names are important clues as 'how we began' and, if there is one, the Domesday description can be used. If lists of medieval trades survive, these can be compared with modern industries; trade surnames can be listed and discussed; population figures can be used. The theme of *change* can be a focal one: why did new people come; why did old trades and industries decline and new ones take their place; why did houses change, and shops? A local castle, monastery or other ancient monument would, of course, partly shape this topic. The group can begin to distinguish styles of ecclesiastical and secular architecture.

ACTIVITIES
Making a map of important natural features
Making a series of picture-maps or plans to show how the community grew, or models to show it at various stages
Drawing pictures of buildings and making an architectural book
Writing and illustrating a history of the community
Writing a history of any local famous men or women
Making a list of local street and place names and their meanings

BOOKS
For the pupil
See those suggested under 1.1.1, local histories, newspapers, guidebooks and also:
Rudge, K., *Man Makes Towns,* Start Books, Hamish Hamilton.
Tutley, P., *Discovering Local History,* Look and Remember History, Book V, Allman & Son.

For the teacher
The Concise Oxford Dictionary of English Place-names, Clarendon Press, Oxford.

AUDIO-VISUAL MATERIAL
Some typical buildings in a village, Slide Centre. 12 colour slides with notes
Things seen in a village, Slide Centre. 12 colour slides with notes.
The development of the domestic house, Slide Centre. 3 sets of slides with notes.
Old industrial towns, Slide Centre. 12 black and white slides with notes.
Transition to modern planning, Slide Centre. 12 slides with notes.

2.1.2 *Social Life in our community 50/100/200 years ago*
Context can be broader than for 1.1.2, including the lives of different sorts of family, their work, their play, their troubles, leading into the social life of a whole community, with contrasts between rich and poor. Special topics might include contrasts between kitchens then and now, domestic service, working conditions in shop or factory, water supply and sanitation. Thus an introduction can be given to the social problems with which our forefathers struggled.

ACTIVITIES
Visiting a local museum to make drawings and notes on relevant exhibits, recording dates carefully.
Making a frieze of social life at one or more moments in time
Making a costume and furniture book for one or more periods
Making a glossary of new words (e.g. technical terms for furniture)
Mounting a book of contrasts between Then and Now
Playing children's games of the period and singing the songs
Acting scenes in the home, school and street
Discussing whether you would rather live Then or Now

BOOKS
For the pupil
See those suggested under 1.1.2 and also:
Bowood, R., *The Story of Houses and Homes,* Ladybird.
Cocke, C., *Houses and Homes,* Macdonald.
Delgado, A., *Edwardian England,* Then and There, Longman.
Delgado, A., *A Hundred Years of Medical Care,* Then and There, Longman.
Harrison, M. and Royston, O., *Picture Source Book for Social History, late nineteenth century,* Allen & Unwin.
Hunter, E., *The Story of Furniture,* Ladybird.
Matthews, C. M., *How Place-names Began,* Lutterworth Press.
Speed, P. F., *Learning and Teaching in Victorian Times,* Then and There, Longman.

Taylor, R., *Homes*, Brockhampton Press.
Unstead, R. J., *A History of Houses*, Black.
Watson, R., *Edwin Chadwick, Poor Law and Public Health*, Then and There, Longman.

For the teacher
Opie, I. and P., *Children's Games in Street and Playground*, Oxford University Press.
Opie, I. and P., *The Oxford Dictionary of Nursery Rhymes*, Oxford University Press.

AUDIO-VISUAL MATERIAL
Victorian Social Life, G. Avery, Longman/Common Ground. Set of 4 colour filmstrips with notes

2.2 **Topics of difference**

2.2.1 *Prehistoric men*

This topic now moves beyond playing at being stone-age men. The focus can be on bronze-age and iron-age men and the beginning of settled community life and early technology (food-growing and storing, house-building, evolution of tools, metal-work, pottery, weaving). Burial customs, monuments, earthworks can be introduced. Local archaeological finds can be used to introduce the group to the exciting ways in which archaeologists find out about early people and to the whole idea of finding out through following clues. Alternatively it would be stimulating to put the emphasis on ancient African cultures as leading in 'stone-age progress' and at later stages too.

ACTIVITIES
Making plans of local prehistoric sites and drawings of exhibits in the local museum.
Making a set of drawings or a chart to show the development of tools
Making drawings or models to show burials and monuments (e.g. a burial barrow, Stonehenge, Avebury)
Writing and illustrating an adventure story about bronze- or iron-age people
Comparing an imaginary primitive rubbish dump with a modern one and discussing what we find out about them and ourselves from such evidence
Discussing what was the most important invention or discovery made by early men

BOOKS

For the pupil

See those suggested under 1.2.1 and also:

Ceram, C. W., *Archaeology*, The Odyssey Library, Hamlyn.

Cleator, P. E., *Archaeology*, True Books, Muller.

Goff, C., *Archaeology*, Macdonald.

Goff, C., *Prehistoric Life*, Macdonald.

Higham, C., *Life in the Old Stone Age*, Introduction to the History of Mankind, Cambridge University Press.

Mellersh, H. E. L., *Finding out about Stone Age Britain*, Experiencing the Past, Muller.

Neurath, M. and Turner, M., *They Lived Like This in the Old Stone Age*, Macdonald.

Shepherd, W., *Archaeology*, Young Scientists, Weidenfeld & Nicolson.

White, A., *All about Archaeology*, W. H. Allen.

For the teacher

Davidson, B., *Discovering Africa's Past*, Longman.

Woolley, L., *History Unearthed*, Benn.

AUDIO-VISUAL MATERIAL

Prehistory, T. Cairns and C. Meynell, Oxford University Press. 20 slides with notes.

Prehistory, Slide Centre. 8 colour slides with notes.

Early man, Jordanhill College of Education History Working Party, Scottish Centre for Social Subjects. Kit containing teacher's guide, filmstrip, worksheets, factsheets.

Stonehenge, Slide Centre. 2 sets of slides with notes.

Prehistoric buildings in Britain, Slide Centre. 12 colour slides with notes.

West Kennet long barrow, Slide Centre. 6 colour slides with notes.

Living Before History, M. Neurath, Longman/Common Ground. Set of 3 colour filmstrips with notes.

2.2.2 *A topic on one of the ancient civilisations*

This could be either an enlargement of a topic already suggested or a new patch.

i. *Ancient Babylon*   Beginning with the Sumerians, then Hammurabi and his law code, then later Babylon.

ii. *Ancient Crete and Homeric Greece*   Using the rich material from excavations and the legends of Theseus and the Minotaur, the Trojan War, Ulysses. The story of deciphering the Cretan inscriptions has the excitement of cracking a code. In both these topics the experiences of archaeologists (Woolley, Schliemann, Evans) make a fascinating story.

ACTIVITIES

Making drawings and models

Illustrating legends (e.g. Theseus tracking the Minotaur, the Trojan
Horse, Ulysses and Polyphemus

Language work on new words

Dramatising a story, such as those mentioned above

Writing an account of one of the excavations as if you had taken part
in it

BOOKS

For the pupil

Bolton, J., *Ancient Crete and Mycenae*, Then and There, Longman.

Jones, J. E., *The Greeks*, The Young Archaeologist Books, Hart-Davis.

Neurath, M. and Warboys, W., *They Lived Like This in Ancient
Mesopotamia*, Macdonald.

Pike, E. R., *Finding Out About the Babylonians*, Exploring the Past,
Muller.

Pike, E. R., *Finding Out About the Minoans*, Muller.

Sheppard, E. J., *Babylon and Jerusalem*, Then and There, Longman.

Woolley, L., *Digging up the Past*, Penguin.

Woolley, L., *History Unearthed*, Benn (see bibliography in this).

AUDIO-VISUAL MATERIAL

The Ancient World, E. J. Sheppard, Then and There, Longman/Com-
mon Ground (see above).

The Ancient Greeks, Slide Centre. 16 colour slides with notes.

Life in Ancient Greece, C. A. Stott, Longman/Common Ground.
Colour filmstrip with notes.

Crete: The Minoan age, Time Life. Colour filmstrip with captions.

iii. *Alexander's Empire*   Here, instead of legendary figures, we have
heroic deeds of actual men in an adventure of conquest that took them
to the ends of the known world.

ACTIVITIES

Mapping Alexander's marches and conquests right to India, working
out roughly in miles or kilometres how far he went

Telling the story of your adventures with Alexander as one of his
soldiers

Drawing pictures or making models of Greek soldiers and their
weapons

Painting pictures, e.g. Alexander taming Bucephalus, his army
marching through the desert

BOOKS
For the pupil
Dance, E. H., *Alexander the Great,* Men of Mark, Hutchinson.
Mitchison, N., *Alexander the Great,* Then and There, Longman.

For the teacher
Breasted, J., *Ancient Times,* Ginn.
Woolley, L., *History Unearthed,* Benn (see bibliography to this).

AUDIO-VISUAL MATERIAL
The Ancient World, E. J. Sheppard, Then and There, Longman/Common Ground (see above).
Alexander the Great, L. du Garde Peach, Ladybird. Colour filmstrip.

iv. *Ancient China*   Introducing the group to a remote but fascinating civilisation where people were discovering things and making inventions long before we in the West did.

ACTIVITIES
Finding out about China geographically and making a map
Making a chart to compare life in the West with China under its early great dynasties
Making a frieze of Chinese life in the style of Chinese painting
Discussing the differences between ancient Chinese ideas and Western ones

BOOKS
For the pupil
Barrett, G., *Ancient China,* Then and There, Longman.
Burland, C. A., *Ancient China,* Hulton.
Morrison, I. A., *China,* Ladybird.
Nancarrow, P., *Early China and the Wall,* Introduction to the Study of Mankind, Topic Book, Cambridge University Press.
Sauvain, P. A., *The Great Wall of China,* Round the World Histories, Hulton.
Spencer, C., *Ancient China,* Young Historian, Weidenfeld & Nicolson.
Taylor, B., *China,* Brockhampton Press.

For the teacher
Creel, H., *The Birth of China,* Cape.

AUDIO-VISUAL MATERIAL
China; the Han and T'ang dynasties, K. Pratt, Visual Publications.
  Colour filmstrip with notes.
China: a cultural heritage, Jackdaw no. 140, Jackdaw Publications.

v. *Ancient India* Particularly if the group includes Indians or
Pakistanis, an exploration of the ancient civilisation of the Indus
Valley (Mohenjo-Daro) and then the development of Hindu culture,
with some of its famous temples and sculptures, perhaps in south
India, would be exciting.

ACTIVITIES
Similar to those suggested under iv. above

BOOKS
For the pupil, these are difficult to find
Neurath, M. and Ellis, J., *They Lived Like This in Ancient India*,
  Macdonald.

For the teacher
Woolley, L., *History Unearthed*, Benn.

AUDIO-VISUAL MATERIAL
The city of Mohenjo-Daro, Macmillan History Wallcharts, no. 14,
  Macmillan.

2.2.3 *Topics already suggested*
i. *Ancient Egypt* This could now be focused successively on (a) the
Old Empire and the Pyramids (b) Akenhaten and Tutankhamun.
The Pharaohs' government, beliefs about the world, the gods, the
after-life (see Akenhaten's special beliefs), can all be explored more
fully. The full story of the discovery of Tutankhamun's tomb and its
splendid furniture can be used.

ACTIVITIES
See those suggested under 1.2.2
Drawing pictures of Akenhaten and his family
Writing a story about Princess Nefertiti
Reading aloud Akenhaten's 'Hymn to the Sun' or lettering it with
  pictures
Telling an eye-witness story of the opening of Tutankhamun's tomb

BOOKS
For the pupil
See those suggested under 1.2.2 and also:
Allen, A., *The Story of Archaeology*, Faber.
Boase, W., *Ancient Egypt*, Scimitar, Closer Look Books.
Burland, C. A., *Ancient Egypt*, Peoples of the Past, Hunton.
Burland, C. A., *The Egyptians*, Macdonald.
Sellman, R., *Ancient Egypt*, Arnold.
Sewell, B. and Lynch, P., *Ancient Egypt*, Arnold.
Stewart, P. and Davies, P., *Tutankhamun's Egypt*. Wayland.

For the teacher
Casson, L., *Ancient Egypt*, Time Life International.
Fox. P., *Tutankhamun's Treasure*, Oxford University Press.
Murray, M., *The Splendour That Was Egypt*, Sidgwick & Jackson.

AUDIO-VISUAL MATERIAL
The Ancient World, E. J. Sheppard, Then and There, Longman/Common Ground (see above).
Egypt, The Slide Centre. 8 colour slides with notes.
Life in Ancient Egypt, M. Neurath, Longman/Common Ground. Colour filmstrip with notes.
Treasures of Tutankhamun, Rainbird. 12 colour slides with notes.
Tutankhamun and the discovery of the tomb, M. Magnusson, Jackdaw no. 124, Jackdaw Publications.
Wall painting from the tomb of Nebamun, Thebes 1400 BC, British Museum. Wallchart.

ii. *Athens in the fifth century*   If not already taken, this can now be a full topic on social life in ancient Greece, centring on Athens in her hey-day and contrasted with Sparta. Besides aspects suggested under 1.2.3, the triumph over the Persians (stories from Herodotus), the Delian League as a peace method, the great Athenian building programme (optical illusions used in building the Parthenon), the Panathenea and other festivals, plays (comedies and tragedies), the Olympic games and government can all be explored.

ACTIVITIES
See those suggested under 1.2.3
Making a plan of Athens
Drawing or making models of great buildings
Writing stories about the Persian Wars (e.g. Pheidippides the runner or holding the pass at Thermopylae), or competing in the Olympic games, or taking part in the great procession

Language work on words we get from the Greek

Making a short comic play about Athenian people: this might follow a
   reading of short pieces from Aristophanes' comedies and the group
   might then have a chorus of frogs, birds or wasps in their play

Discussing which was best – Athenian or Spartan education

Discussing whether you would rather live Then or Now

BOOKS

For the pupil

See those under 1.2.3 and also:

Anderson, P., *Finding Out about the Athenians*, Muller.

Barker, D., *Story of Ancient Greece*, Arnold.

Connolly, P., *The Greek Armies*, Macdonald.

Green, R., *The True Book about Ancient Greece*, Muller.

Lewis, B., *Greek Myth and Legend*, Wayland.

Sheppard, E., *Ancient Athens*, Then and There, Longman.

Taylor, B., *Ancient Greeks*, Brockhampton Press.

Whittle, T., *The World of Classical Greece*, Heinemann.

For the teacher

Boardman, J., *Greek Art*, Thames & Hudson.

Translations of Herodotus' *History* and Aristophanes' comedies in
   Everyman editions.

AUDIO-VISUAL MATERIAL

Greek architecture, J. Doulton. Nicholas Hunter. Colour filmstrip with
   notes.

iii. *Ancient Rome or Roman Britain* The topic can be shifted to
whichever focus was not used before. There is good material on the
Romans in Scotland and Wales, as well as England. More emphasis
can be placed on military conquests, army organisation, a soldier's
life, his armour and weapons, building roads, camps, aqueducts,
Roman towns. Different types of villa (adapted to climate) can be
studied. How the Romans governed their great empire can be
discussed and even the great question of why they failed to keep it.

ACTIVITIES

See those suggested under 1.2.3

Making your own map of the Roman Empire and/or Roman Britain

Writing the story or diary of a Roman boy who becomes a soldier

Giving talks on Roman methods of fighting, being a Roman citizen,
   Roman Law

Writing a story or play about living in Pompeii and the eruption of
  Vesuvius, or living on the Roman Wall in north Britain
Mounting an exhibition of Roman life
Listing the Roman names for important places in Britain
Discussing whether, if you were barbarians, you would rather be
  conquered and brought inside the Empire, or remain outside

BOOKS
For the pupil
See those suggested under 1.2.3 and also:
Allen, K., *One Day in Roman Britain*, Tyndall.
Burrell, R. E. C., *The Romans in Britain*, Wheaton.
Connolly, P., *The Roman Army*, Macdonald.
Connolly, P., *The Romans*, Peoples of the Past, Macdonald.
Forman, J., *The Romans*, Peoples of the Past, Macdonald.
Grant, M. and Pottinger, D., *Romans*, Nelson.
Hodges, H. and Pyddoke, E., *Ancient Britons*, John Baker.
Jamieson, J. M., *The Romans in Britain*, Arnold.
Liversidge, J., *Roman Britain*, Then and There, Longman.
Liversidge, J., *Roman Gaul*, Then and There, Longman.
Lobban, R. D., *Roman Britain*, Quest Library, Oliver & Boyd.
Mitchell, R., *Roman Britain*, Focus on History, Longman.
Nicholls, R. and McLeish, K., *Through Roman Eyes*, Cambridge
  University Press
Place, R., *The Celts*, Peoples of the Past, Macdonald.
Sauvain, P., *Roman Britain*, Imagining the Past, Macmillan.
Sherwin-White, N., *Ancient Rome*, Then and There, Longman.
Taylor, B., *Ancient Romans*, Brockhampton Press.
Taylor, B., *Early Britain*, Brockhampton Press.
Taylor, D., *A Soldier on Hadrian's Wall*, People of the Past, Oxford
  University Press.
Thomson, O., *The Romans in Scotland*, Then and There, Longman.
Titley, P., *The Roman World*, Look & Remember, Mills & Boon.
Unstead, R. J., *See Inside a Roman Town*, Hutchinson.
White, V., *A Romano-British Family*, People of the Past, Oxford
  University Press.
Whittle, T., *Imperial Rome*, Heinemann.
Ancient Britain, Macdonald Junior Reference Library, Macdonald.

For the teacher
Carcopino, J., *Daily Life in Ancient Rome*, Penguin.
Raven, S., *Rome in Africa*, Evans.
Wheeler, M., *Roman Art and Architecture*, Thames and Hudson.
Cowell, F. R., *Everyday Life in Ancient Rome*, Batsford.

AUDIO-VISUAL MATERIAL
Ancient Rome, Gateway. Colour filmstrip with notes.
The Roman house, Education Audio-Visual. Colour filmstrip with
   notes.
Pompeii, Gateway. Colour filmstrip with notes.
The Romans, C. L. Hammer, Educational Productions. Colour
   filmstrip with notes.
Life in the Roman Empire, C. A. Stott, Longman/Common Ground.
   Colour filmstrip with notes.
Verulamium: a Romano-British town, M. Kane, Studio Two. 16 colour
   slides with notes and cassette.
Life in Roman Britain, Slide Centre. 16 colour slides with notes.
The Roman occupation, Gateway. 2 colour filmstrips with notes.
The Romans came this way, British Transport Films. Colour filmstrip
   with notes.

2.2.4 *Alfred and the Danes*

If the Viking topic has been taken, this can concentrate on the Viking
attack on Wessex. Extracts from the Anglo-Saxon Chronicle can be
used to build up the grim tale of ravaging, chasing, fighting, Alfred's
response to the challenge and the climax of his victory at Ethandun in
878. Life in Anglo-Saxon Wessex can be studied from contemporary
rural pictures, Alfred's Laws and Aelfric's *Colloquies.* Alfred's
achievements as a monarch of peace lead to the question of what was
most needed to build a peaceful society after war years. The move
from bloodfeud to 'wergild' in Anglo-Saxon society makes a good
point. The positive side of the Vikings – their beautiful artefacts,
trade, social organisation – needs stressing and their legacy to Britain,
e.g. in language.

ACTIVITIES
Making your own map of Viking raids on Britain and their
   settlements
Making a chronicle of Alfred's fight, in the style of the Anglo-Saxon
   Chronicle
Making an imaginary picture of the Battle of Ethandun; this could be
   a big composite one by the whole group
Making a play about Alfred and the Danes
Painting a frieze of Anglo-Saxon and Viking people
Giving talks, e.g. on the Alfred Jewel, legends about Alfred, the White
   Horses
Lettering some of Alfred's Laws on a wall-sheet
Acting a scene in the Witan when they were making laws

Language work on words we get from Scandinavia

Discussing why Alfred wanted people to be able to read and why he translated books for them

Writing what you think about Alfred as if you were either Bishop Asser or Guthrum the Dane

BOOKS

For the pupil

See those suggested under 1.2.4 and also:

Anderson, J. R. L., *The Vikings*, Kestrel Books.

Blyth, J., *King Alfred the Saxon Leader*, The Way It Was, Chambers.

Boucher, A., *A Viking Raider*, People of the Past, Oxford University Press.

Burland, C. A., *The Vikings*, Hulton.

Dickinson Rich, L., *The First Book of the Vikings*, Franklin Watts.

Jamieson, J. M., *Saxon and Viking Britain*, Arnold.

Lobban, R. D., *The Vikings*, English Universities Press.

Middleton, G., *Saxon and Viking Britain*, Arnold.

Neurath, M. and Ellis, J., *The Vikings*, Macdonald.

Phillips-Birt, D., *Finding Out About the Vikings*, Muller.

Reeves, M., *Alfred and the Danes*, Then and There, Longman.

Roberts, M., *Fury of the Vikings*, The Way It Was, Chambers.

Sellman, R., *The Anglo-Saxons*, Methuen.

Simpson, J., *Everyday Life in the Viking Age*, Carousel Books.

Simpson, J., *The Vikings*, Peoples of the Past, Macdonald.

Taylor, B., *Saxons, Vikings and Normans*, Brockhampton Press.

For the teacher

Quennell, M. and C. H. B., *Everyday Life in Roman and Anglo Saxon Times*, Batsford.

Whitelocke, D. (ed.), *English Historical Documents*, Eyre & Spottiswoode.

The Anglo-Saxon Chronicle, Everyman, Dent.

AUDIO-VISUAL MATERIAL

Alfred the Great: his life and times, Slide Centre. 16 colour slides with notes.

Alfred the Great, D. Johnson, Jackdaw no. 89, Jackdaw Publications.

Life in Anglo-Saxon times, Slide Centre. 16 colour slides with notes.

The Saxons, Visual Publications. Colour filmstrip with notes.

2.2.5 *The Norman Conquest*

An exciting narrative can be built up from chronicles and the Bayeux Tapestry. For discussion: why William came, what mistakes Harold made, why the English gave up fighting and why William won. How a conqueror dealt with a conquered land (cf. today), leads on to the Domesday Survey: if your locality is recorded, your public library should supply an English version of the survey. Scottish groups can focus on the Normans in Scotland and Welsh groups on the Marcher lords and their castles.

ACTIVITIES

Making a map to show William's marches and the centres of resistance

Making a frieze of the Battle of Hastings in the style of the Bayeux Tapestry

Writing the story of the Battle of Hastings from the viewpoint of either one of William's or one of Harold's soldiers

Acting scenes, e.g. Harold taking the oath to William, the comet and Edward the Confessor's death, waiting for a wind to cross the Channel, the English surrender in London, William's coronation

Acting or writing the story of Hereward the Wake

Acting scenes from the making of Domesday Book

Making your own Domesday Survey of all the homes in your group or of your own village/locality

Discussing (a) which side you would have been on – Harold's or William's (b) whether William was a good or bad king

BOOKS

For the pupil

Coltham, J. B. and Wright, W. H., *Norman Times*, Life Then, Hart-Davis.

Crowther, N. and Carstairs, I., *The Norman Conquest*, Action History, Arnold.

Osler, D., *Queen Margaret of Scotland*, The Way It Was, Chambers.

Reeves, M., *The Norman Conquest*, Then and There, Longman.

Ritchie, W. K., *Scotland and the Normans*, Then and There, Longman.

Rooke, P., *The Normans*, Macdonald.

Scarfe, N., *Norman England*, Focus on History, Longman.

Taylor, B., *Saxons, Vikings and Normans*, Brockhampton Press.

Turner, J., *King David I of Scotland, A Medieval King*, The Way It Was, Chambers.

For the teacher

Douglas, D. C. (ed.), *English Historical Documents*, Eyre & Spottiswoode.

Kingsley, C., *Hereward the Wake* (any edition).

Stenton, F. M., *The Bayeux Tapestry*, Phaidon.

AUDIO-VISUAL MATERIAL

Bayeux tapestry, S. M. Newton, Visual Publications. 2 colour filmstrips with notes.

Life in Norman England, Slide Centre. 16 colour slides with notes.

The Norman invasion, C. W. E. Peckett, Visual Publications. Colour filmstrip with notes.

William the Conqueror: his life and times, Slide Centre. 16 colour slides with notes.

2.2.6 *Medieval life*

This is the great moment for re-enacting the life of medieval communities which offer exciting 'differences' and colourful detail in a basically intelligible context. Individual role-play in different 'jobs' and group acting of community activities suggest themselves. Of four possible foci, each carrying a wealth of detail in written and pictorial sources, one could well last three to four weeks, but all four could be dealt with more superficially. Scottish and Welsh children could find a local focus.

i. *Life in a medieval village*   The basic necessities and tasks of an agricultural community, its work-year, its problems, laws and punishments, its games and festivals.

ii. *Life in a medieval town*   If possible, identified with a local town, its trades, guilds and their regulations, markets and fairs, government, games, festivals, including medieval plays.

iii. *Life in a medieval castle*   If possible, focused on a local castle, emphasising strategic sites, castle-building, methods of attack and defence, training squires and knights, armour, heraldry, tournaments, women's occupations, feasts, stories of chivalry and exploits, e.g. of William the Marshal or legendary ones, e.g. Arthurian knights or Gawain and the Green Knight.

iv. *Life in a medieval monastery*   The most difficult of these communities to enter into because of its religious dimension, hence much sympathetic imagination is needed. If possible, use a local religious house, studying the different members of the monastery, its layout, the monastic day, training novices, making books.

ACTIVITIES

For all there are various forms of rôle-play which can develop into plays.

Making plans or models of village, town, castle or monastery

Making a calendar with pictures of the village year or a time-table of the monastic day

Drawing plans of different types of castle or pictures to illustrate different siege weapons

Drawing a series of pictures to show the development of armour, labelled with the correct technical terms

Making a glossary of technical terms for any one topic

Making an illustrated guide to heraldry

Painting imaginary scenes in these different communities

Mounting an exhibition to illustrate life in one of them

Making rules for the village and acting a manor-court scene, or making guild or town rules and punishing culprits who break them

Lettering a psalm and illuminating it with little scenes in the style of a medieval psalter

Writing a story, e.g. of a village thief, a runaway serf who gets rich in a town, a knight in a tournament or battle, a boy who becomes a novice and then a monk

Acting stories of King Arthur and Sir Gawain

BOOKS FOR THE PUPIL

Bailey, V. and Wise, E., *Medieval Life*, Focus on History, Longman.

Davies, P., *Growing Up in the Middle Ages; Town Life in the Middle Ages; Country Life in the Middle Ages*, Wayland.

Gass, I., *A Glance at Heraldry*, Harrap.

Hunter, E., *Arms and Armour*, Ladybird Achievement Book, Ladybird.

Jeffreys, S., *A Medieval Siege*, Wayland Sentinel.

Lobban, R. D., *Medieval Life*, Quest Library, Oliver & Boyd.

Mitchell, R. J., *The Medieval Feast*, Then and There, Longman.

Mitchell, R. J., *The Medieval Tournament*, Then and There, Longman.

Moncrieffe, I. and Pottinger, D., *Simple Heraldry*, Nelson.

Priestley, A. E., *Heraldry*, Ladybird.

Reeves, M., *The Medieval Village; The Medieval Town; The Medieval Castle; The Medieval Monastery*, Then and There, Longman.

Ritchie, W. K., *Scotland and the Normans*, Then and There, Longman.

Ritchie, W. K., *Scotland in the Time of Wallace and Bruce*, Then and There, Longman.

Sauvain, P., *A Medieval Town; A Castle; An Abbey*, Imagining the Past, Macmillan.

Sayers, T., *Life in a Medieval Monastery*, Focus on History, Longman.

Taylor, B., *Middle Ages; Castles and Fortifications; Arms and Armour*, Brockhampton Press.

Unstead, R. J., *Castles*, Macdonald.

Unstead, R. J., *Monasteries; Castles*, Black.

Unstead, R. J., *See Inside a Castle*, Hutchinson.

Wilkins, F., *Castles*, Blackwell's Learning Library, Blackwell.

Arms and Armour, Picture Reference Book, Brockhampton Press.

AUDIO-VISUAL MATERIAL

The Castle, E. K. Milliken, Longman/Common Ground. Colour filmstrip with notes.

The Cistercian Abbey: Rievaulx, H. Whittle, Educational Productions. Colour filmstrip with notes.

The Crusaders, A. C. Green, Longman/Common Ground. Colour filmstrip with notes.

The Knight, G. E. P. Sidaway, Longman/Common Ground. Colour filmstrip with notes.

The Medieval Town, C. L. Hammer, Educational Productions. Colour filmstrip with notes.

The Medieval World, M. Reeves, Then and There, Longman/Common Ground. Set of 3 colour filmstrips with notes.

The Monastery, E. K. Milliken, Longman/Common Ground. Colour filmstrip with notes.

The Town, A. C. Green, Longman/Common Ground. Colour filmstrip with notes.

The Village, A. C. Green, Longman/Common Ground. Colour filmstrip with notes.

2.2.7 *Adventurers beyond Europe*

Adventures of exploration obviously belong to this stage. In all cases where exploring Europeans were meeting other, sometimes older, civilisations (e.g. Chinese, Mayan and Aztec, Indian, Maori) the wonders of these other peoples can be emphasised and the treasures which Europeans often grabbed and sometimes destroyed. There are rich narrative sources on all the following, from which a selection can be made:

  i. Marco Polo's adventures in travelling to Cathay
 ii. Portuguese adventurers going south and east
iii. Columbus's voyages westward
 iv. The Conquest of Mexico and Peru, focused on Cortes and Pizarro
  v. Some sixteenth-century explorer stories, e.g. Frobisher, Drake, Gilbert, explorers on the coast of Virginia, Barents in the Arctic
 vi. Later stories could include Captain Cook's voyages, explorers of North America (trappers and Red Indians), coming into this century with polar exploration, the conquest of Everest and space exploration.

ACTIVITIES

Making picture maps to illustrate voyages and travels and calculating approximate distances for important expeditions

Making a frieze of different types of ship

Writing an imaginary diary or log of an expedition and illustrating it
Acting scenes, e.g. Marco Polo at the court of Kublai Khan, Columbus's first landing, Cortes in Mexico, episodes in Drake's voyage round the world, explorers meeting Indians in Virginia
Painting imaginary pictures of exciting scenes
Discussing why explorers set out on these perilous adventures and whether it is braver to be a spaceman today than Columbus in the fifteenth century

BOOKS FOR THE PUPIL

Beacroft, B., *The Voyages of Christopher Columbus*, Then and There, Longman.

Bellis, H., *Captain Cook*, Nile & Mackenzie for McGraw Hill, Far Eastern Publications.

Benson, B., *Ships*, Macdonald.

Burland, C. A., *Montezuma, Lord of the Aztecs*, Hulton.

Cowie, L., *The Age of Drake*, Wayland.

de Leeuw, A., *James Cook*, Muller.

Donahue, P., *Plymouth Ho! The West in Elizabethan Times*, Then and There, Longman.

Dorner. J., *Cortes and the Aztecs*, Then and There, Longman.

Francken, D., *Famous Names in World Exploration*, Wayland.

Graves, C. P., *Marco Polo*, Muller.

Groh, L., *Ferdinand Magellan*, Muller.

Hanson, A., *Discovery, The Lives of the People*, Bk. II, Heinemann.

Hart, R., *The Voyages of Captain Cook*, Wayland.

Hope, R., *Ships*, Junior Heritage Series, Batsford.

Kaufman, M. D., *Christopher Columbus*, Muller.

Latham, R., *Marco Polo, Traveller to the East*, Macdonald.

Lobban, R. D., *The Conquistadors*, English Universities Press.

Lonsdale, A., *Merchant Adventurers in the East*, Then and There, Longman.

Pritchard, D. C., *The Early Settlers in Pennsylvania*, Hulton.

Reeves, M., *Explorers of the Elizabethan Age*, Then and There, Longman.

Robinson, G., *Elizabethan Ship*, Then and There, Longman.

Smith, D. and Newton, D., *Exploration; Explorers*, In History, Schofield & Sims.

Stokes, G., *Marco Polo and Cathay*, Then and There, Longman.

Sylvester, D., *Captain Cook and the Pacific*, Then and There, Longman.

Tate, E. N., *Pizarro and the Incas*, Then and There, Longman.

Wodzicka, H., *Ships and Seafarers*, Wayland.

Wymer, N., *Great Explorers*, Oxford University Press.

Famous Explorers, Macdonald Junior Reference Library, Macdonald.

AUDIO-VISUAL MATERIAL

Marco Polo, Beacon Filmstrips. Colour filmstrip with notes.

Marco Polo and Cathay, M. Reeves and A. Lonsdale, Longman/Common Ground. 12 colour slides with notes.

Christopher Columbus, Hulton. Colour filmstrip with notes.

Discovery of North America, Educational Productions. Colour filmstrip with notes.

Drake, Visual Publications. Colour filmstrip with notes.

The sea and an empire, 2: Foundations of Empire, Visual Publications. Black and white filmstrip with notes.

The search for a sea route to India: the Portuguese Navigators, Educational Productions. Black and white filmstrip with notes.

Sir Walter Raleigh, L. du Garde Peach, Ladybird. Colour filmstrip.

Captain Cook of the Pacific, BBC Radiovision. Colour filmstrip with notes to accompany radio broadcast in 'Arts and Humanities' series. (Designed for 13–16 year olds.)

Captain Cook's second voyage, Woodmansterne/National Maritime Museum. 9 Colour slides.

Cook, A. C. Green, Visual Publications. Colour filmstrip with notes.

Cook's second voyage, BBC Radiovision. Colour filmstrip with notes to accompany radio broadcast in 'World History' series.

Cortes and the Aztecs, J. Dorner, Longman/Common Ground. 12 colour slides with notes.

Inca civilisation, Slide Centre. 16 colour slides with notes.

The Age of Discovery and Exploration, M. Reeves and A. Lonsdale, Longman/Common Ground. Set of 3 colour filmstrips with notes.

2.3 Threads to trace

  i. If not already taken, the development of transport and communications comes well here, with more specialised treatment

  ii. Clothes through the ages, related to climate and function

  iii. House-building through the ages

  iv. Farming through the ages

  v. Symbols and flags, starting from heraldry and moving to the evolution of national flags and other symbols

ACTIVITIES

Time-charts or picture friezes to show developments

Models for the same purpose

Mounting an exhibition on one of these topics

Making a book of 'Transport', or 'Clothes' or 'Houses' or 'Heraldry and Flags'

BOOKS FOR THE PUPIL

See those suggested under 1.3.2 and 2.2.6 and also:

Addy, J., *The Agrarian Revolution,* Then and There, Longman.

Barfoot, A., *Discovering Costume,* University of London Press.

Barford, A., *Homes in Britain,* Batsford.

Binder, P., *Look at Clothes,* School Look Book, Hamilton.

Bucknall, R., *Trains,* Macdonald.

Cunnington, P., *Costume,* Black.

Drummond, J. and Mackay, J., *Clothes,* People at Work, Chambers.

Eldon, K. and M., *Kitchens and Cooking,* Methuen.

Ellacott, S., *The Story of the Kitchen,* Methuen.

Greenwood, M., *The Railway Revolution,* Then and There, Longman.

Greenwood, M., *Roads and Canals in the Eighteenth Century,* Then and There, Longman.

Hanson, A., *Work and Invention,* The Lives of the People, Heinemann.

Harvey, J., *Fashion and Clothes,* Macdonald.

Healey, T., *History of Costume,* Macdonald.

Hope, R., *Ships,* Junior Heritage, Batsford.

Laver, J., *Dress,* John Murray.

Lewenhak, S., *Steamships and Shipbuilders in the Industrial Revolution,* Then and There, Longman.

Osmond, E., *Houses,* Junior Heritage, Batsford.

Potter, M. and A., *Houses,* John Murray.

Redmayne, P., *Britain's Food,* John Murray.

Redmayne, P., *Transport by Land; Air; Sea,* John Murray.

Schofield, A., *Clothes in History,* Wayland.

Taylor, B., *Costume,* Brockhampton Press.

Udin, G., *They Looked Like This,* Blackwell.

Unstead, R. J., *A History of Houses,* Black.

Wyatt, R., *Cars,* Macdonald.

3 The secondary stage: the first two years (ages about 11–13)

3.1 The study of ourselves

3.1.1 *Our own town/locality*

There is much overlap between this stage and the previous one, and since the group will probably be coming from a variety of schools, a general topic on 'our community', as outlined in 2.1.1, may be new to many of them. Content and activities can be much the same as above, but with more statistical work, e.g. on population, trades, etc., more on local resources and their influence on industry, perhaps more on architecture and buildings. More precisely, the focus could be on *local religious life*, churches, synagogues, temples, and what goes on in them. This would be particularly valuable in a multi-racial area where it is important that different religious communities should understand each other.

Another possibility is the study of *local amusements*, past and present. The public library or museum may have collections of old playbills and newspapers advertising entertainments; there may still be an old theatre or music-hall. The history of local sports and their clubs, or local fairs may be worth investigating.

ACTIVITIES

Visits to churches, other old buildings, monuments, graveyards, museums and libraries to collect data

Individual assignments, reporting investigations to the group, e.g. of war memorials or graveyards, of trades, of local actors or comedians, of different religions

Discussion on the beliefs of different religious groups

Presentation of a concert programme in costume of period songs and recitations, or of a local fair

BOOKS FOR THE PUPIL

In addition to local material see those books suggested under 2.1.1 and 2.1.2 and also:

Hay, G., *Architecture in Scotland*, Oriel Press.

Rowland, K., *The Shape of Towns*, Looking and Seeing, Ginn.

West, T., *History of Architecture in England*, University of London Press.

Men and Manners: An Anthology of Social History, Macmillan.

3.1.2 *The history of popular education, local and national*

This can start from the first local schools and the lessons taught in them and widen out into the reasons why schools for all developed and how they were run. Local school log-books and old photographs may be available to give a picture of life in an Edwardian or Victorian school.

ACTIVITIES

Writing the story of a day at school in either Victorian or Edwardian times, from the viewpoint of a boy or girl

Writing a play about children fifty or a hundred years ago

Discussing the curriculum in early schools and the advantages and disadvantages of the monitor system

Discussing the contrasts between schools Then and Now

BOOKS FOR THE PUPIL
Dures, A., *Schools*, Batsford.
Speed, P. F. *Learning and Teaching in Victorian Times*, Then and There, Longman.
Wood, R., *Children, 1715-1890*, Evans.

AUDIO-VISUAL MATERIAL
Schools through the ages: ancient Greece to eighteenth century, Slide Centre. 12 colour slides with notes.
Late nineteenth century Board and Charity schools in London, Slide Centre. 12 colour slides with notes.

3.1.3 *Life in Victorian/Edwardian England*
All this could widen out into a broader study of Victorian or Edwardian England: people at work, keeping Sunday, sanitation and water, crime and disease, amusements.

ACTIVITIES
Individual assignments on special topics, reporting to the group
Mounting an exhibition or display of pictures illustrating specific aspects, e.g. working conditions, housing, epidemics, crime
Writing and illustrating an imaginary newspaper or magazine of the period, including advertisements
Making a collection of old advertisements
Writing and acting scenes from the period in costume
Making a Then and Now book of contrasts
Discussing some social problems, e.g. bad housing and 'gin palaces', punishments for crime, accidents and disease caused by work

BOOKS FOR THE PUPIL
Allen, E., *Victorian Children*, Black.
Brash, R. W., *Glasgow in the Tramway Age*, Then and There, Longman.
Delgado, A., *Edwardian England*, Then and There, Longman.
Delgado, A., *A Hundred Years of Medical Care*, Then and There, Longman.
Ferguson, S., *Growing Up in Victorian Britain*, Batsford.
Hughes, J., *A Victorian Sunday*, Wayland.
Speed, P. F., *Police and Prisons*, Then and There, Longman.
Thomas, D., *The Motor Revolution*, Then and There, Longman.
Watson, R., *Edwin Chadwick, Poor Law and Public Health*, Then and There, Longman.
Yglesias, J., *London Life and the Great Exhibition, 1851*, Then and There, Longman.

AUDIO-VISUAL MATERIAL

Life in Edwardian England, Slide Centre. 4 sets of colour slides with notes.

The poor in late Victorian London, Slide Centre. 3 sets of black and white slides with notes.

Street life in the 1870s, Educational Productions. Black and white filmstrip with notes. (Original photographs taken in 1870s.)

Victorian London, Slide Centre. 12 black and white slides with notes.

Victorian Social Life, G. Avery, Longman/Common Ground. Set of 4 colour filmstrips with notes.

3.2 Topics of difference

In the first year many topics suggested under 2.2 are suitable and it will be useful to pick up one or two medieval topics as a starting point. To these can be added:

3.2.1 *The Muslim world and the Crusades*

The topic should start from the story of Mohammed and the astonishing spread of Islamic conquests and culture, moving then to the threat posed by Islam to Christendom and its response in the Crusades. Besides splendid stories of adventure, this topic includes a study of the motives of feudal knights at a more subtle level than before. Religious ardour mingles with greed, ambition and bloodthirstiness. There are vivid chronicle sources for the Council of Clermont (1095), the People's Crusade, the Knights' Crusade and the capture of Jerusalem. Then a jump can be made to the Third Crusade, Richard Coeur de Lion's adventures, the noble enemy, Saladin, and the reasons for the Crusade's failure. At this stage one can discuss, not only mixed motives, but questions of right and wrong in warfare, the idea of the 'just' war and how to deal with noble enemies such as Saladin. Discussions could end with problems of present-day Israel and the Muslim population of Palestine.

ACTIVITIES

Mapping (a) the spread of Islam (b) crusading routes

Dramatising crusading scenes, e.g. the Council of Clermont, Peter the Hermit preaching, Anna Comnena's disgust at Western manners, an imaginary meeting between Richard and Saladin

BOOKS

For the pupil

Bailey, V. and Wise, E., *The Crusades,* Focus on History, Longman.

Bailey, V. and Wise, E., *Mohammed: His Times and Influence,* The Way

It Was, Chambers.

Bailey, V. and Wise, E., *Pilgrimages and Crusades*, The Way It Was, Chambers.

Booth, A. H., *The Great Religions*, Muller.

Brett, B., *Mohammed*, Collins.

Cowie, E. and Craig, G., *Man and the Crusades*, Star Books, Hamish Hamilton.

Gibson, M., *Knights and the Crusades*, Macdonald.

Gittings, J. G., *The Crusades*, Hulton.

Holden, M., *The Crusades*, Wayland.

Kay, S., *The Arab World*, Oxford Children's Reference Library, Oxford University Press.

Lobban, R. D., *The Crusades*, University of London Press.

McWilliam, H. O. A., *Constantinople and the Byzantines*, Then and There, Longman.

McWilliam, H. O. A., *Muhammad and the World of Islam*, Then and There, Longman.

Sellman, R. R., *The Crusades*, Methuen.

Thomas, J., *The Crusades*, Muller.

Townson, D., *Muslim Spain*, Introduction to the History of Mankind, Cambridge University Press.

Treece, H., *Know About the Crusades*, Blackie.

Unstead, R. J., *Living in a Crusader Land*, Black.

Williams, A., *The Crusades*, Then and There, Longman.

For the teacher
Lewis, B., *Islam*, Wayland.

AUDIO-VISUAL MATERIAL

The Crusades, G. Hindley, Education Audio-Visual. 2 colour filmstrips with notes and cassette.

The Crusades, A. C. Green, Longman/Common Ground. Colour filmstrip with notes.

Muhammad and the World of Islam, H. O. A. McWilliam, Longman/Common Ground. 12 colour slides with notes.

Constantinople and the Byzantines, H. O. A. McWilliam, Longman/Common Ground. 12 colour slides with notes.

3.2.2 *Chaucer's England*

The topic of Chaucer and his Canterbury pilgrims gives a vivid picture of England in the fourteenth century. From the pilgrims, exploration broadens out into the lives of the knightly class, the religious, the scholar, the lower classes, while the setting introduces the question of shrines and pilgrimages.

ACTIVITIES

Individual assignments and talks to the group on St Thomas Becket
and his shrine, other famous places of pilgrimage, Chaucer's life

Making a frieze of the pilgrims or a set of models, using the Ellesmere
pictures as guides

Writing and acting a conversation among the pilgrims as they ride

Miming the various characters, while the group guesses who they are

Writing descriptions of some modern people, if possible in verse, in
imitation of Chaucer, and illustrating them

Discussing why people went on pilgrimage and which characters
Chaucer liked best

BOOKS

For the pupil

Bailey, V. and Wise, E., *Medieval Life*, Focus on History, Longman.

Hall, D. J. (ed.), *Topics in Medieval History*, Arnold.

Jeffreys, S., *Tourney and Joust*, Wayland Sentinel.

Ridgard, I., *Dame Alice de Bryene: Life in a Medieval Household*, The Way
It Was, Chambers.

Scott Thomson, G., *Medieval Pilgrimage*, Then and There, Longman.

Serraillier, I., *Chaucer and His World*, Lutterworth Press.

Taylor, D., *Chaucer's England*, Dennis Dobson.

For the teacher

Brewer, D. S., *Chaucer in His Time*, Longman.

AUDIO-VISUAL MATERIAL

Chaucer's England, Slide Centre. 12 colour slides with notes.

Chaucer's pilgrims from the Canterbury Tales, BBC Radiovision. Colour
filmstrip with notes to accompany radio broadcast in 'Living
Language' series.

The Medieval World, M. Reeves, Then and There, Longman/Common
Ground. 3 colour filmstrips with notes.

The time, the life and works of Geoffrey Chaucer, Education Audio-Visual.
Colour filmstrip with notes and cassette.

3.2.3 *Changes in medieval society and the Peasants' Revolt*

This presupposes some knowledge of topics under 2.2.6. The
emphasis is now on change: the impact of the Black Death, a restless
peasantry and artisan class, wandering preachers stirring up
discontent. The climax is the Peasants' Revolt of 1381. The whole
dramatic story can be told in some detail, especially the encounters
with Richard II and the tragic betrayals by king and nobles
afterwards.

ACTIVITIES

Making a map to illustrate the Peasants' Revolt

Writing an eye-witness account of the Black Death coming to a village or the story of a runaway peasant, or the coming of a Poll-Tax collector to a village, or the adventures of a rebel in Wat Tyler's company

Writing a sermon by John Ball or the speech of Richard II to the rebels

Dramatising scenes from the revolt

Writing and acting an argument between a land-owner and a peasant

Discussing why the people wanted freedom and whether they won anything by revolt

BOOKS FOR THE PUPIL

Crowther, N. and Shofields, R., *The Peasants' Revolt*, Arnold.

Davies, P., *Growing up in Medieval Times*, Batsford.

Hobbs, M., *One Day in Medieval England*, Tyndall.

Kesteven, G., *The Peasants' Revolt*, Chatto & Windus.

Lane, P., *The Middle Ages*, Visual History, Batsford.

Lindsay, J., *Nine Days' Hero: Wat Tyler*, Dennis Dobson.

Price, M., *The Peasants' Revolt*, Then and There, Longman.

Turner, D., *The Black Death*, Then and There, Longman.

AUDIO-VISUAL MATERIAL

Plantagenet London, Educational Productions. Black and white filmstrip with notes.

3.2.4 *Tudor England, particularly under Elizabeth I*

Although some early Tudor background is needed, the best focus is on Elizabethan England: the Queen and Court, London life in a country mansion, village life, enclosures and the problems of the poor, rogues and vagabonds. Both the colourful and wretched aspects must find a place. Beyond these lie more detailed aspects: Shakespeare and the theatre, Elizabethan music, dancing pageants and festivities, the Reformation in England, the Queen and her people, the problem of Mary, Queen of Scots, the Spanish danger and the Armada. Pictorial material is rich and short extracts from sources can be used, e.g. Elizabeth's speeches, poems in her honour, Elizabethan plays, descriptions of country life and festivities. Scottish groups can focus on Mary Stuart and the Welsh can view the Tudors as springing from Wales.

ACTIVITIES

Making a Tudor family tree, perhaps with pictures

Individual assignments, reporting to the group on famous Elizabethans, e.g. Sir Walter Raleigh, Sir Philip Sidney, William Cecil

Making an Elizabethan book under such headings as homes, town and country life, clothes, food, amusements, the Queen, great men

Making a series of pictures to show Elizabeth going 'on progress'

Collecting or drawing a series of pictures of Elizabethan costume, houses, furniture and writing notes on them

Writing an eye-witness description of Elizabeth at court, or walking through the London streets, or watching a play at the Globe

Writing and acting an imaginary scene between Elizabeth and Raleigh or Elizabeth and Mary, Queen of Scots

Acting a Christmas festival, with Mummers, the Lord of Misrule, St George and the Dragon

Drawing a picture map to show how the Armada was destroyed

Writing songs and poems, e.g. on Elizabeth (Gloriana) or the defeat of the Armada

Learning some Elizabethan songs and listening to records of their music

Writing and acting a dialogue between a JP and a vagabond

Making models of the Globe, Old London Bridge, ships, costume figures

Mounting an exhibition on the Elizabethan world

BOOKS

For the pupil

Bradbury, J., *Shakespeare and his Theatre*, Then and There, Longman.

Cowie, L., *The Age of Drake*, Wayland.

Davies, K., *Henry Percy and Henry VIII,*Then and There, Longman.

Dodd, A., *Life in Elizabethan England*, Batsford.

Donahue, P., *Plymouth Ho! The West in Elizabethan Times*, Then and There, Longman.

Fincham, P., *Tudor Country Life*, Focus on History, Longman.

Fincham, P., *Tudor Town and Court Life*, Focus on History, Longman.

Fines, J., *Tudor People*, Batsford.

Fletcher, A., *Elizabethan Village*, Then and There, Longman.

Garnett, E., *The Tudors*, Black.

Goyder, R., *A Reformation Family*, Then and There, Longman.

Gray, P., *The Invincible Armada*, McGraw Hill.

Harrison, M. and Bryant, M. E., *Picture Source Book for Social History*, Allen & Unwin.

Holwood, W., *Sir Francis Drake*, Muller.

Kendall, A., *Elizabeth I*, Wayland.

Kesteven, G., *The Armada*, Chatto & Windus.

Kesteven, G., *The Reformation in England*, Chatto & Windus.

Lobban, R. D., *The Elizabethans*, University of London Press.

Mitchell, A., *The Tudor Family*, Wayland.

Neurath, M. and Turner, M., *They Lived Like This in Shakespeare's England*, Macdonald.

Pearce, P. (ed.), *The Sixteenth Century*, Peoples of the Past, Oxford University Press.

Plowden, A., *Elizabeth I*, Harrap.

Reeves, M., *Elizabethan Court*, Then and There, Longman.

Reeves, M., *Explorers of the Elizabethan Age*, Then and There, Longman.

Reeves, M. and Hodgson, P., *Elizabethan Citizen*, Then and There, Longman.

Ritchie, W. K., *Mary, Queen of Scots and the Scottish Reformation*, Then and There, Longman.

Sellman, R. R., *The Elizabethan Seamen*, Methuen.

Taylor, D., *The Elizabethan Age*, Dennis Dobson.

For the teacher
Strong, R. and Oman, J., *Elizabeth R.*, Secker & Warburg.

AUDIO-VISUAL MATERIAL

Drake, Visual Publications. Colour filmstrip with notes.

Life in Elizabethan England, Slide Centre. 4 sets of colour slides with notes.

Life in Tudor England, Slide Centre. 4 sets of colour slides with notes.

Portrait of a family: the Tudors, Encyclopaedia Britannica. 5 colour filmstrips with notes.

The Spanish Armada, Encyclopaedia Britannica. Colour filmstrip with captions.

The time, the life, the works of William Shakespeare, Education Audio-Visual. Colour filmstrip with notes and cassette.

The World of the Tudors, M. Reeves, Then and There, Longman/Common Ground. Filmstrip with booklet of source material.

Life in Tudor Times, A. L. Dahl, Longman/Common Ground. Colour filmstrip with notes.

3.2.5 *Cavaliers and Roundheads*

This is a vital political theme of English History but it can be treated in the context of one or more Stuart families, particularly one in which the family split between the two sides. Against the background of social life, the causes of the Civil War can be traced through members attending parliament, the arguments on taking sides can be thrashed out and family tragedies and hardships through battles, sieges and escapes can be dramatically told. Thus the basic political issues should be imaginatively understood as principles for which people fought and died. In Scotland the focus can be partly on the Covenanters.

ACTIVITIES

If possible, visiting a Stuart house or museum

Individual assignments, reporting to the group, on the great figures, e.g. Charles I, John Hampden, Cromwell

Collecting or drawing pictures of Stuart costume, armour, houses, furniture and writing notes on them

Writing the diary of a young MP who finally joins the side opposite to his family side and fights in the war

Writing an imaginary speech in Parliament by Cromwell or another of the leaders

Writing and acting a family argument over which side to join

Drawing maps to show the movements of the two armies and perhaps a more detailed one to show the war in the school locality

Writing imaginary letters which passed between a Cavalier or Roundhead soldier and his wife or sisters at home

Staging a debate in Parliament on whether to execute the King, or staging the actual trial of Charles I

Writing an escape story of a Cavalier family

Holding a parliamentary debate on whether it was safe to give freedom to Radicals like the Diggers

Discussing why they fought, whether the war was necessary, whether it was right to execute the King and which side members of the group would have taken

BOOKS FOR THE PUPIL

Bailey, V. and Wise, E., *The Early Stuarts and the Civil War*, Focus on History, Longman.

Blakeway, M., *A Roundhead Soldier*, People of the Past, Oxford University Press.

Cowie, L., *Trial and Execution of Charles I*, Wayland.

Gibson, M., *Cavaliers and Roundheads*, Wayland.

Harrison, M. and Wells, A., *Picture Source Book: Seventeenth Century*, Allen & Unwin.

Kesteven, G., *The Execution of the King*, Chatto & Windus.

Murphy, E., *Cavaliers and Roundheads*, Then and There, Longman.

Reeve, J. and Millward, J., *Portraits and Documents: The Seventeenth Century*, Hutchinson.

Ritchie, W. K., *Scotland in the Time of the Covenanters*, Then and There, Longman.
Sellman, R. R., *Civil War and the Commonwealth*, Methuen.
Taylor, B., *Early Stuarts (1603–1660)*, Brockhampton Press.
Titley, P., *Tudors and Stuarts*, Allman & Son.
Woolrych, A., *Oliver Cromwell*, Clarendon Biographies, Oxford University Press.
Wroughton, J., *Cromwell and the Roundheads*, Macmillan.

AUDIO-VISUAL MATERIAL
Life in Stuart England, Slide Centre. 4 sets of colour slides with notes.
Oliver Cromwell, Slide Centre. 16 colour slides with notes.
England in the Seventeenth Century, H. Cubitt, Longman/Common Ground. 4 filmstrips with notes.
Life in Early Stuart Times, A. L. Dahl, Longman/Common Ground. Colour filmstrip with notes.

3.2.6 *Mr Pepys in London*
Here there is a great bonus of being able to stand in the shoes of a vivid diarist, and so view the London scene in the second half of the seventeenth century, and especially the dramatic events of the Plague and Great Fire, followed by the rebuilding of London. Besides Pepys' diary, there are many contemporary pictures, buildings, objects, costumes and songs.

ACTIVITIES
Visiting a museum or a late Stuart house and making a collection of pictures to illustrate costume, houses, furniture and so on
Making a map of Pepys' London
Writing a diary in the Pepysian style of experiences in the time of the Plague and Fire
Painting a series of pictures to illustrate the Great Fire
Finding out about Sir Christopher Wren, if possible visiting St Paul's and other Wren churches
Drawing a series of pictures to illustrate Wren architecture
Making a Stuart book of pictures, descriptions and stories
Discussing why the plague had died out by 1700 in England, why Wren could not carry out all his plans for rebuilding London and whether we did any better when another opportunity to rebuild London came at the end of the Second World War

BOOKS FOR THE PUPIL
Gibson, J. (ed.), *Selections from the Diaries of John Evelyn and Samuel Pepys*, Chatto & Windus.

Gray, P., *Plague and Fire*, McGraw Hill.

Hawke-Genn, J., *A Doctor at the Time of the Plague*, People of the Past, Oxford University Press.

Middleton, G., *At the Time of the Plague and the Fire*, Focus on History, Longman.

Murphy, E., *Samuel Pepys in London*, Then and There, Longman.

Taylor, B., *Later Stuarts*, Brockhampton Press.

Turner, D., *The Black Death* (seventeenth-century parts), Then and There, Longman.

Wodzicka, *The Glorious Age of Charles II*, Wayland.

AUDIO-VISUAL MATERIAL

The diary of Samuel Pepys, read by Ian Richardson, Caedmon, 1976, Cassette.

Life in Restoration times, Longman/Common Ground, 1968. Colour filmstrip with notes.

Pepys' London, Education Audio-Visual. Colour filmstrip with notes and cassette.

England in the seventeenth century, H. Cubitt, Then and There, Longman/Common Ground. 4 filmstrips with notes.

3.2.7 *British and French in North America*

This topic would pick up from the explorer theme and develop into a study of the various reasons why Europeans wanted to settle in North America, what sort of people made good colonists, what problems they met, how they treated the Indians, how their government developed and how the English colonists clashed with the home government. It culminates in the conquest of Canada by Britain (see the dramatic story of Quebec) and the American Revolution. It can be studied in practical, concrete terms of the life of colonists and yet form an introduction to the British Empire and its problems.

ACTIVITIES

Making a picture-map (in sixteenth-century style) of the colonisation of North America

Individual assignments, with talks to the group, on different Red Indian tribes, famous explorers, American leaders in the Revolution

Writing the diary of an early colonist, in Virginia or New England

Writing a letter to the home government, e.g. from Virginia, with urgent demands for supplies, tools, carpenters, farmers, builders, etc.

Holding a council to make laws for a new colony

Writing adventure stories, e.g. colonists captured by Indians, experiences of a wife who emigrated with her husband, hunting buffalo

Writing the story of Princess Pocahontas, as told by herself

Drawing a set of pictures of Indians, animals, fruits, etc. in the style of John White

Writing the diary of a soldier to show the stages in the conquest of Canada

Dramatising the Boston Tea-Party

Holding a debate between the Loyalists and Revolutionaries in America

Studying and discussing the Declaration of Independence

Discussing what sent colonists across the Atlantic, had they any right to dispossess the Indians, why was it difficult to govern colonies from home, were the Americans right to revolt?

BOOKS FOR THE PUPIL

Barker, A. J. *Redcoats: The British Soldier in America*, Dent.

Claridge, J., *The Discovery of America*, Usborne Publishing.

Collins, B., *The Mayflower Pilgrims*, Wayland.

Clarke, C., *The American Revolution*, Then and There, Longman.

Clarke, C., *The Young American Republic*, Then and There, Longman.

Currie, B., *Gold Miners in the American West*, Then and There, Longman.

Currie, B., *The Last Fighting Indians of the American West*, Then and There, Longman.

Currie, B., *Pioneers in the American West*, Then and There, Longman.

Gill, W., *Captain John Smith and Virginia*, Then and There, Longman.

Gill, W., *The Pilgrim Fathers*, Then and There, Longman.

James, L. F., *A Settler in New England*, People of the Past, Oxford University Press.

Nolan, F. W., *The Pilgrim Fathers*, Macdonald.

Parkinson, R., *The American Revolution*, Wayland.

Pritchard, D. C., *The Early Settlers in Pennsylvania*, Hulton.

Unstead, R. J., *Emerging Empire*, Macdonald.

Williams, B., *The Struggle for Canada*, Then and There, Longman.

AUDIO-VISUAL MATERIAL

Discovery of North America, P. Wenham, Educational Productions. Colour filmstrip with notes.

The sea and an empire, part 4: Struggle with France (B) America. Visual Publications. Black and white filmstrip with notes.

Early America: the Indians and the First Settlers, B. Beacroft, Longman/Common Ground. Colour filmstrip with notes.

The Westward Movement, B. Beacroft, Longman/Common Ground. Colour filmstrip with notes.

3.2.8 *The wonders of India and intruding Europeans*

This starts with India, its geography and the wonders of its ancient Hindu culture. Reference can be made back to topic 2.2.2. If the group includes children whose families come from India or Pakistan they might give information on family and social life, religious practices and so on. The topic moves to the rich Moghul empire in India where there is splendid pictorial material on the Red Forts of Agra and Delhi, the Taj Mahal and other royal tombs and the royal residence at Fati-pur-Sikri. Here the focus can be on Akbar. Then the intruding merchants, Portuguese, French, British, can be introduced, leading to the story of Clive in India. Finally the question can be debated as to why the British came to rule India, whether there was any justification for this rule and what legacies Britain has left to India today.

ACTIVITIES

Individual assignment leading to talks on the different peoples of India, or its three great religions or some of its great monuments and paintings

Making maps to show (a) India before the advent of Europeans (b) the chief powers in India in the seventeenth and eighteenth centuries

Making a collection of pictures to show the magnificence of Hindu and Moghul art and buildings

Painting a series of pictures in the Indian style, e.g. an elephant hunt, Akbar and his court, ladies in a garden

Staging the debate between Akbar and a Muslim, a Christian and a Buddhist in his palace

Mounting an exhibition of Indian culture

Writing the diary of a European merchant in India in the seventeenth or early eighteenth century

Writing letters home from Clive telling of his experiences

Writing an eye-witness account of the Black Hole of Calcutta

Discussing the questions suggested above

Finding out more about India today

BOOKS FOR THE PUPIL

Harrison, J., *Akbar and the Mughal Empire*, Harrap.

Judd, D., *The British Raj*, Wayland.

Sylvester, D., *Clive of India*, Then and There, Longman.
Zinkin, T., *India and Her Neighbours*, Oxford Children's Reference Library, Oxford University Press.

AUDIO-VISUAL MATERIAL
The sea and an empire, part 3: Struggle with France (A) India, Visual Publications. Black and white filmstrip with notes.

3.2.9 *Change in England during the eighteenth and early nineteenth centuries*
The focus can be on agrarian or industrial aspects of change, according to the locality of the school, with the emphasis first on technical developments to meet economic demands and how one invention led to another, and then on the social consequences for employers and workers, especially working conditions, child labour and housing. There is a good deal of source material to use.

ACTIVITIES
Making a chart of developments in one or more aspects, e.g. textiles, mining, metallurgy, pottery, agriculture
Individual assignments and talks on specific inventions, with diagrams or models
Writing an argument between a peasant farmer and a rich landowner
Writing a story about work in the mines or the troubles of a weaver's family or a child working in a factory
Preparing evidence for and then staging the meeting of a Royal Commission to investigate working conditions either in factories or mines (evidence to be given by both workers and employers); having heard the evidence, the group as a whole could draw up a Factory or Mines Bill of reforms to be presented to Parliament
Discussing whether, in the long run, these great changes were good or bad in their results

BOOKS FOR THE PUPIL
Addy, J., *The Agrarian Revolution*, Then and There, Longman.
Addy, J., *A Coal and Iron Community in the Industrial Revolution*, Then and There, Longman.
Archer, S., *Josiah Wedgwood and the Potteries*, Then and There, Longman.
Barrie, A., *The Railway Builders*, Wayland.
Blakeway, M., *A Canal Builder*, People of the Past, Oxford University Press.
Cummings, H., *Early Railways*, Macdonald.

Davies, P., *Children of the Industrial Revolution*, Wayland.

Donnachie, I., *Roads and Canals 1700–1900*, Scottish Search, Holmes McDougall.

Dorking, J. W., *Men and Machines*, Oliver & Boyd.

Ellacott, S., *Forge and Foundry*, Methuen.

Ellacott, S., *Spinning and Weaving*, Methuen.

Fyson, N. L., *Growing Up in the Eighteenth Century*, Batsford.

Hanson, A., *Work and Invention*, The Lives of the People, Heinemann.

Hogg, A. and McIver, M., *Industry – Coal and Iron 1700–1900*, Scottish Search, Holmes McDougall.

Lawton, F., *The Machine Makers*, Macdonald.

McKechnie, K., *A Border Woollen Town in the Industrial Revolution*, Then and There, Longman.

McKichan, F., *The Highland Clearances*, Then and There, Longman.

Power, E. G., *A Textile Community in the Industrial Revolution*, Then and There, Longman.

Shapiro, H., *Scotland in the Days of Burns*, Then and There, Longman.

Simpson, E. and Tate, E. N., *Farming and the Countryside 1700–1900*, Scottish Search, Holmes McDougall.

Skipp, V., *An Eighteenth-Century Farm Labourer's Family*, People of the Past, Oxford University Press.

Taylor, B., *Machines*; *Georgians*, Brockhampton Press.

Tolley, B., *Liverpool and the American Cotton Trade*, Then and There, Longman.

Tomalin, N., *Coal, Mines and Miners*, Methuen.

Tomalin, N., *Growth of Mechanical Power*, Methuen.

Whately, R., *An Eighteenth-Century Toll-Keeper*, People of the Past, Oxford University Press.

Wymer, N., *Great Inventions*, Oxford University Press.

Yglesias, J. R. C., *Georgian England*, Focus on History, Longman.

SOURCE BOOKS
For the pupil
Addy, J. and Power, K. E. (eds), *The Industrial Revolution*, Longman.

Cameron, A. D., *Living in Scotland 1760–1820*, Oliver & Boyd.

Ross, A. C., *Changing Scotland 1760–1820*, Longman.

For the teacher
Royston Pike, E., *Human Documents of Adam Smith's Time*, Allen & Unwin.

Royston Pike, E., *Human Documents of the Industrial Revolution*, Allen & Unwin.

AUDIO-VISUAL MATERIAL
The Age of Steam, BBC. Songs and documentary material.
The Industrial Revolution, J. Addy and E. G. Power, Longman/Common
  Ground. 4 filmstrips with notes.
The Industrial Revolution: child labour, Slide Centre. 18 slides with notes.
The Agrarian Revolution, J. Addy and G. Ruffhead, Longman/Common
  Ground. 3 filmstrips with notes.

3.2.10 *Europeans in the Far East and explorers in the Pacific*
This topic includes the story of how the British 'barbarians' broke
into China and secured Hong Kong and also the exploration of the
Pacific and the colonisation of Australia and New Zealand. The
accounts of British embassies to China, by both Chinese and British,
and the records of Captain Cook's voyages are the chief literary
sources, but the rich material on Chinese art and culture and the
remains of Maori culture are important.

ACTIVITIES
Mapping explorers' routes in the east
Individual assignments on geographical factors, Chinese art, Chinese
  inventions, Confucius, the culture of the Maori
Learning and writing some Chinese characters
Studying and discussing Chinese painting, porcelain, jade and
  bronze figures and silks
Writing letters home from one of the first British embassies to China
Staging a scene in which the Emperor finally receives a British
  embassy
Painting a series of pictures in the Chinese style of the first British
  travelling to Peking
Discussing (a) the opium problem and whether the British were
  wrong in the opium wars (b) why the Chinese were so conservative
  and how the old empire contrasts with China today
Finding out about Hong Kong today
Mounting an exhibition of Chinese things
Writing a log, with illustrations, of one or more of Cook's voyages
Writing a story about emigrating to Australia in the early days or
  about the gold rush in Australia

BOOKS FOR THE PUPIL
Adams, K. N., *The First Australians*, Seeing History, Angus &
  Robertson.
Barr, P., *Foreign Devils*, Penguin.
Gibson, M., *China: Opium Wars to Revolution*, Wayland.

Grant, A., *Sailing Ships and Emigrants in Victorian Times*, Then and There, Longman.

Hart, R., *Voyages of Captain Cook*, Wayland.

Hobley, L., *Exploring the Pacific*, Methuen.

Lonsdale, A., *China*, Oxford Children's Reference Library, Oxford University Press.

Lonsdale, A., *Merchant Adventurers in the East*, Then and There, Longman.

Musman, R., *Captain Cook*, Hutchinson.

Pownall, E., *Exploring Australia*, Methuen.

Pratt, K., *Peking in the early seventeenth century*, Oxford University Press.

Stokes, G. and J., *Barbarians in Peking*, Then and There, Longman.

Sylvester, D. W., *Captain Cook and the Pacific*, Then and There, Longman.

Unstead, R. J. and Henderson, W. F., *Pioneer Home Life in Australia*, Black.

AUDIO-VISUAL MATERIAL

A convict's tour of hell, Round and Round Cassettes, Educational Media Australia. Cassette – excerpts from accounts of early European settlers in Australia.

The great Australian legend, arranged by A. L. Lloyd, Topic Records. Record of songs and ballads.

3.2.11 *Discovering Africa*

The first focus should be on Africa itself, its vastness, the greatness of its past empires and the mysteries surrounding some of them through the absence of written records. Many clues are now being found in buildings and objects dug up, in legends and stories, in the lives of people today. The great empires are probably too many to study (e.g. Zimbabwe, ancient Ghana in the Sudan, Mali, the Swahili peoples, the Shona, Benin), so the focus could be on one region, emphasising the stubborn battle to tame the natural surroundings and use their resources. The group can then move on to nineteenth-century explorers who came in for a variety of motives – genuine curiosity, missionary zeal and the lure of wealth – leading, on one side, to the great missionary enterprise and, on the other, to the scramble of European powers for land. Here the 'outsiders' should be balanced by the African heroes of modern times (e.g. Khama of Botswana, Aggrey of West Africa). Finally, without too much political detail, problems of Africa today can be raised, with discussions on how much harm was done by European exploiters and how black and white inhabitants could live peaceably together today.

ACTIVITIES
Similar to previous topics

BOOKS FOR THE PUPIL
Addison, J., *Ancient Africa*, Hart-Davis.
Arnold, R., *David Livingstone*, Muller.
Barker, C., *The Oba of Benin*, Macdonald & Jane's.
Davidson, B., *Discovering Africa's Past*, Longman.
Gibbs, P., *Cecil Rhodes*, Muller.
Hall, R., *Explorers in Africa*, Museum of Discovery, Usborne
    Publishing.
Hobley, L., *Opening Africa*, Methuen.
Hollyer, B., *The Slave Trade*, Macdonald.
Judd, D., *Livingstone in Africa*, Wayland.
Martin, B., *John Newton and the Slave Trade*, Then and There,
    Longman.
McClelland, E. M., *The Kingdom of Benin in the Sixteenth Century*, Oxford
    University Press.
McKown, R., *The Colonial Conquest of Africa*, Franklin Watts.
Mountfield, A., *The Slave Trade*, Wayland.
Neurath, M. and Warboys, E., *They Lived Like This in Ancient Africa*,
    Max Parrish.
Ritchie, W. K., *The British in Egypt*, Then and There, Longman.
Sharman, M., *Africa Through the Ages*, Evans.
Sterling, T., *Exploration of Africa*, Cassell Caravel.
Tames, R. L. A., *Cecil Rhodes*, Lifeline, Shire Publications.
Tames, R. L. A., *General Gordon*, Lifeline, Shire Publications.
Tames, R. L. A., *Henry Morton Stanley*, Lifeline, Shire Publications.
Tames, R. L. A., *Mungo Park*, Shire Publications.
Wymer, N., *Great Explorers*, Oxford University Press.

AUDIO-VISUAL MATERIAL
The Arts of Africa, Visual Publications. Filmstrips with notes.
The story of the Zulus, Slide Centre. 12 colour slides with notes.
David Livingstone, Visual Publications. Colour filmstrips with notes.

3.3 **Threads to trace**

3.3.1 *Technical inventions leading to social change*
If not taken before there are various themes:
  i. evolution of agricultural tools and machinery from primitive hoes
     and ploughs to combine harvesters
  ii. evolution of textile methods and machinery

iii. development of mining methods and machinery
iv. history of books, printing, newspapers. This leads to discussions on the importance of spreading information, what we have gained by the printing press, what the dangers of a 'free press' are, why governments have tried to control it in the past and whether we need censorship today.

ACTIVITIES
As with other 'thread' topics, making evolutionary charts, or a series of models or pictures to show developments. An exhibition could be staged on one or more developments, with an explanatory guide booklet. Discussions will turn on the social gains and losses of various inventions.

BOOKS FOR THE PUPIL
See those suggested under 2.3 and 3.2.9 and also:
Bear, J., *Communications*, Macdonald.
Ellacott, S., *Forge and Foundry*, Methuen.
Ellacott, S., *Spinning and Weaving*, Methuen.
Hanson, A., *Work and Invention*, The Lives of the People, Heinemann.
Huggett, F., *Newspapers*, Muller.
James, A., *Newspapers and The Times in the Nineteenth Century*, Then and There, Longman.
Larsen, E., *Inventions*, Muller.
Morgan, T. J., *Television and Radio*, Muller.
Redmayne, P. and Insull, T. (eds), *The Changing Shape of Things* (series), John Murray.
Roberts, D., *Bicycles and Motorcycles*, Museum of Discovery, Usborne Publishing.
Robertson, E. C., *Jet Engines*, Muller.
Tomalin, N., *Coal Mines and Miners*, Methuen.
Tomalin, N., *Growth of Mechanical Power*, Methuen.
Wadzick, H., *The Printer and his Craft*, Wayland.

4 The secondary stage: the second two years (ages about 13–15)

4.1 About ourselves

4.1.1 *How we learned to govern ourselves*
The basic problem of government can first be studied in the medieval situation in a simpler, more direct form than in more complex modern situations. The first focus can, for example, be on twelfth-century

government, where the workings of the Exchequer, the development of law-courts, methods of trial leading to the jury system and the King's methods of checking corruption in his officials can be studied in a practical way. A discussion of Magna Carta and its purposes follows. Then the focus can shift to the growth of Parliament in the thirteenth and fourteenth centuries: why people were summoned, who they were, what they did and why the powers of Parliament grew. Emphasis should be on practical problems and how rulers and their servants tried to solve them, rather than on institutions in the abstract. Tudor ways of making government stronger after fifteenth-century disorders – by prerogative law in special courts and the use of JPs – and then the clash between royal and parliamentary concepts of government in the seventeenth century, can all be set against the background of knowledge from previous topics. For modern times a selection of themes must be made, e.g. the emergence of Cabinet government, the independence of the judiciary, parliamentary reform down to universal suffrage, the development of the modern party system. A continuing theme for discussion is how, in successive stages, men have tried to balance the need for strong government against the claims of individual and group freedom, ending with discussion on the chief problems of government today.

ACTIVITIES

Charts: (a) to show various organs of government developing from medieval times (b) to show the extension of the franchise to all

Dramatisation: (a) a session of the Exchequer Court to check sheriffs' accounts (b) King John and the barons at Runnymede (c) a meeting of the medieval shire-court to choose MPs for Parliament (d) Elizabeth addressing her Parliament (e) a parliamentary debate in the reign of Charles I (f) Charles I comes to arrest the five members

Debates or discussion: (a) whether the jury system was a better method of trial than ordeal or trial by battle (b) the respective merits of Tudor prerogative courts (e.g. Star Chamber) and common law courts (c) why Elizabeth I could 'get round' her parliaments (d) for and against the independence of the judiciary (e) for and against our present party system

Argumentative writing: (a) is strong government more important than individual freedom? (b) the case for Charles I against Parliament or vice versa (c) a defence or attack on the Suffragette movement

Imaginative writing: (a) an eye-witness account of trial by ordeal or battle (b) a letter home from an MP describing Elizabeth I in Parliament (c) an eye-witness account of a parliamentary election before 1832 (d) a suffragette's diary

BOOKS FOR THE PUPIL

Addy, J., *Parliamentary Elections and Reforms*, Then and There, Longman.

Holt, J., *Magna Carta*, Then and There, Longman.

Lane, P., *Elections*, Batsford.

Liversidge, D., *Parliament*, Franklin Watts.

Mackenzie, T., *Parliament*, Methuen.

McNichol, M., *Scotland and the Union*, Then and There, Longman.

Murphy, E., *Roundheads and Cavaliers*, Then and There, Longman.

Palmer, M. D., *Government*, Batsford.

Prentice, D. M., *Your Book of Parliament*, Faber.

Reeves, M., *A Medieval King Governs*, Then and There, Longman.

Ritchie, W. K., *Scotland in the Time of the Covenanters*, Then and There, Longman.

Rooke, P., *Parliament*, Wayland.

Shapiro, H., *John Wilkes and Parliament*, Then and There, Longman.

Smith, D. and Newton, D., *Government*, In History, Schofield & Sims.

Snellgrove, L., *Suffragettes and Votes for Women*, Then and There, Longman.

Wymer, N., *Behind the Scenes in Parliament*, Phoenix House.

AUDIO-VISUAL MATERIAL

People and parliament, 1603–1928, Studio Two. 16 slides with notes and tape recording.

Jackdaws: no. 3, *Magna Carta*; no. 16, *The Vote 1832–1928*; no. 17, *Peterloo and Radical reform*; no. 125, *The Budget*, Jackdaw Publications.

4.1.2 *How workers organised themselves – a history of the Trade Union Movement and the Parliamentary Labour Party*

This topic can begin by recalling previous knowledge of medieval guilds, then move to the history of local workers' movements, and then out into the national field. The focus can be first on the personalities, the struggles and the dedication of individual leaders and what they sacrificed for the cause, moving then to a study of the various methods used, their successes and failures, and finally to the crucial question of whether to work through Parliament or to go for direct economic action in strikes. Francis Place, Robert Owen, the Chartists, the Tolpuddle Martyrs, the Rebecca Riots, Keir Hardie, the General Strike, will obviously provide some of the highlights. There may be good local detail and there is some vivid autobiographical material.

ACTIVITIES

Individual assignments: (a) on famous worker-leaders and (b) on local worker activities (strikes, protests, pamphlets and hand-bills)

Charts: (a) the progress of the Trade Union Movement (b) the progress of the Parliamentary Labour Party

Dramatisation: (a) a strike meeting in connection with a specific strike (e.g. a local one, the Great Dock Strike, the General Strike) (b) the Chartist March (c) Keir Hardie taking his seat in Parliament

Debates or discussions: (a) why the Chartist Movement failed (b) who was the greatest worker-leader? (c) which was the most important, the growth of Trade Unionism or of the Parliamentary Labour Party?

Argumentative and imaginative writing: (a) production of a workers' newspaper (b) composition of manifestoes, posters or songs of protest in connection with a particular workers' campaign (c) an imaginary autobiography of a worker-leader in a particular industry (d) a letter home from a worker who was punished by transportation (e) a Chartist speech (f) an eye-witness account of the great Chartist March

BOOKS FOR THE PUPIL

See those suggested under 3.2.9 and also:

Cootes, R., *The General Strike*, Then and There, Longman.

Lobban, R. D., *Employment*, Batsford.

Lobban, R. D., *The Trades Unions – A Short History*, Sources of History, Macmillan.

Northcote, C., *A Docker Goes on Strike*, People of the Past, Oxford University Press.

Robertson, A., *The Trade Unions*, Hamish Hamilton.

Rooke, P., *The Trade Union Movement*, Wayland.

Searby, P., *The Chartists*, Then and There, Longman.

Searby, P., *Weavers and Outworkers in Victorian Times*, Then and There, Longman.

Shapiro, H., *Keir Hardie and the Labour Party*, Then and There, Longman.

Wasp, D. and Davis, A., *The Great Dock Strike*, Then and There, Longman.

Wilmot, E. P., *The Labour Party – A Short History*, Sources of History, Macmillan.

SOURCE BOOKS

Addy, J. and Power, E., *The Industrial Revolution*, Longman.

AUDIO-VISUAL MATERIAL

Poverty, organised labour and the state, 1870–1970, Nicholas Hunter. 25 colour slides with notes.

The early Trade Unions, S. Lewenhak, Jackdaw no. 35, Jackdaw Publications.

Unrest, reform and organised labour 1770–1870, David Morgan, Nicholas Hunter. Colour filmstrip with notes.

Trade Union History, Student recordings. Colour filmstrip with notes and cassette.

The General Strike 1926, David & Charles Reprints. Reprints from *British Gazette* and *British Worker* of 1926.

The General Strike, R. Tames, Jackdaw no. 105, Jackdaw Publications.

The Tolpuddle Martyrs, Student recordings. Colour filmstrip with notes.

The Industrial Revolution, J. Addy and E. G. Power, Longman/Common Ground. 4 filmstrips with notes.

4.1.3 *How reformers campaigned to get bad conditions changed*
This is a study of philanthropy and reform through the lives of men and women who dedicated themselves to obtaining justice and rights for disadvantaged groups of people. Some or all of the following can be included:

  i. campaign against slavery led by Wilberforce
 ii. prison reform, particularly the work of John Howard and Elizabeth Fry
iii. reform of conditions in factories, mines and for workers at home with Lord Shaftesbury as a leading figure
 iv. attacks on disease caused by bad sanitation and water supplies, led by Chadwick and others
  v. campaign for cheap bread, led by Cobden and Bright
 vi. campaign for popular education, involving a whole group of educators
vii. reforms in medicine and hospitals

There may be local reformers who took up these or other causes. The emphasis is on the variety of methods used to publicise evils and rouse public opinion; also on the persistent, informed hard work needed to get something done. The point can be made that most reformers were working for other people's interests, not their own, and the topic could end in discussion of possible causes to work for today.

ACTIVITIES
Individual assignments: on lives of reformers, local and national
Compilation of a book: on reformers or reform movements

Dramatisation: (a) Elizabeth Fry visits a prison (b) a Royal Commission hears evidence on work conditions for women and children in textile factories or mines (c) a scene in a school run on the monitorial principle (d) Florence Nightingale inspects a hospital

Imaginative and argumentative writing: (a) a speech for or against the abolition of slavery, or the abolition of the Corn Laws (b) a special edition of a newspaper devoted to exposing a particular evil, e.g. employment of children, disease-breeding slums, state of prisons or hospitals (c) posters denouncing particular evils, e.g. working conditions of match-girls at Bryant and May's works (d) part of an imaginary diary of a reformer, e.g. Elizabeth Fry (e) a school inspector's report on a school for poor children (f) a letter from Florence Nightingale from the army hospital in the Crimea

Analysis: listing and categorising all the different methods used by reformers

Discussion: (a) what methods were most effective? (b) what groups opposed reforms and why? (c) what made reformers work for other people's rights? (d) what kind of reform do we need today?

BOOKS

Bardens, D., *Elizabeth Fry*, Muller.

Briggs, A., *William Cobbett*, Clarendon Biographies, Oxford University Press.

Calder, J. M., *The Story of Nursing*, Methuen.

Delgado, A., *A Hundred Years of Medical Care*, Then and There, Longman.

Delgado, A., *As They Saw Her – Florence Nightingale*, Harrap.

Dorner, J., *Newgate to Tyburn*, Wayland.

Martin, B., *John Newton and the Slave Trade*, Then and There, Longman.

Power, E. G., *Robert Peel, Free Trade and the Corn Laws*, Then and There, Longman.

Walton, J., *Six Reformers*, Oxford University Press.

Wasp, D. and Davis, A., *The Great Dock Strike 1889*, Then and There, Longman.

Watson, R., *Edwin Chadwick, Poor Law and Public Health*, Then and There, Longman.

Wymer, N., *Social Reformers*, Oxford University Press.

AUDIO-VISUAL MATERIAL

Florence Nightingale, Visual Publications. Colour filmstrip with notes.

Shaftesbury and the Working Children, J. Langdon-Davis, Jackdaw No. 7, Jackdaw Publications.

Social Welfare, Longman Secondary History Packs, Longman.

Health and Housing, Batsford history unit, Batsford. 40 workcards, time-chart and teacher's notes.

Elizabeth Fry and Prison Reform, D. Johnson, Jackdaw No. 63, Jackdaw Publications.

Health and Education, 1770–1870, D. Morgan, Nicholas Hunter. Colour filmstrip with notes.

Public Health in the 19th Century, Educational Foundation for Visual Aids. Colour filmstrip with notes.

4.1.4 *Britain and Ireland in the twentieth century*

This is clearly a subject of great tension but therefore all the more necessary to study, with, of course, particular care to present sympathetically the differing points of view, without burking criticism or condemnation where the cause of humanity demands it. With an introduction on the unhappy legacy from the sixteenth and seventeenth centuries, the topic could start with Ireland in the mid-nineteenth century and the disaster of the Potato Famine, passing to the Home Rule movement and so to the state of feelings just prior to the First World War. Then from the Easter Rising events take their inexorable course down to the present tragic situation.

ACTIVITIES

The obvious ones would be imaginative writing of speeches, manifestoes, newspapers, songs, from the viewpoint of one or other side, but probably the subject is too emotionally charged for the encouragement of partisan writing. Debates or discussions on the issues at stake at various moments of crisis can be conducted more objectively, with the emphasis on listening to both sides.

BOOKS

Dures, A., *Modern Ireland*, Wayland.

Fitzgibbon, C., *Out of the Lion's Paw*, Macdonald.

Hawthorne, J. (ed.), *Two Centuries of Irish History*, BBC.

Lane, P., *Ireland*, Batsford.

Power, E. G., *The Easter Rising and Irish Independence*, Then and There, Longman.

Speed, P. F., *The Potato Famine and the Irish Emigrants*, Then and There, Longman.

Tierney, M. and MacCurtain, M., *The Birth of Modern Ireland*, Gill & Macmillan, Dublin.

AUDIO-VISUAL MATERIAL
The Easter Rising: Dublin 1916, A. Comerford. Jackdaw no. 61,
    Jackdaw Publications.
Bloody Sunday, 1972; now called *Whose Point of View*, Education
    Audio-Visual. Colour filmstrip with notes and cassette.

4.1.5 *Britain and the Commonwealth in the twentieth century*
If the exploration themes have been taken up in the previous two
years, the emphasis can now be placed on the ways Britain acquired
rule over various parts of the world, the extent of the empire under
Queen Victoria, the movement for self-government and then
independence, and the emergence of the Commonwealth in the
twentieth century. Discussion can now focus on what holds the
Commonwealth together today, whether it is a force for peace, what
responsibilities we in Britain have towards other peoples of the
Commonwealth, particularly to Commonwealth immigrants and
their descendants who have come to live in Britain.

ACTIVITIES
Individual assignments: on geographical topics concerning different
    parts of the Empire
Maps and charts: to show the growth of the British Empire and the
    stages by which it became the Commonwealth
Dramatisation: scenes from Kipling's or other stories on the Empire
Talks: by members of immigrant families on the family homeland,
    with perhaps slides or photographs (e.g. Jamaica, India, Pakistan)
Collection: of pictures illustrating the Empire and Commonwealth
Imaginative writing: (a) adventure stories, diaries, letters home from
    soldiers or civil servants in various parts of the Empire (b) speeches
    on independence or descriptions of Independence Day, e.g. in
    India or an African state (c) a television programme on one state in
    the Commonwealth
Debates or discussions: on the issues mentioned above

BOOKS FOR THE PUPIL
See those suggested under 3.2.7, 3.2.8, 3.2.11, various stories by
Rudyard Kipling and also:
Blunt, C. H. C., *The Last Hundred Years*, Oxford University Press.
Hobley, L. F., *Britain's Place in the World*, Book 4, Oliver & Boyd.
Howard, R., *Empire to Commonwealth*, Wayland.
McGuffie, T. H., *History for Today*, Books 4 and 5, Macmillan.
Moore, K., *Kipling and the White Man's Burden*, Faber.
Nunn, E., *The Growth of the British Commonwealth*, Ginn.

Rooney, D. D., *The Story of the Commonwealth*, Pergamon.
Turnbull, D., *The Shape of Twentieth-Century Europe*, Book 2, Macmillan.
Williamson, J. A., *Story of the Empire in Pictures*, Odhams.

AUDIO-VISUAL MATERIAL
The Commonwealth Today, 2nd edn., Commonwealth Institute. Folder containing information leaflets, bibliographies, etc.

4.1.6 *Britain and Europe in the twentieth century*
An important aspect of 'ourselves today' is our membership of the European Community, with all the hesitations and differing views about it which British people hold. But the path to membership lies through two world wars which I have placed under 4.2.2 below (Some great 'moments' in European and World history). This should be studied first and then, out of the Second World War experiences, there arises the idea of the EEC as originally conceived by Robert Schuman and the question of British involvement. This gives a chance to bring home how the last war radically changed Britain's position and how the disappearance of the Empire forced us to re-think our relation to our closest neighbours in Europe. The course of the debate can be followed from initial refusal to hesitant membership and some practical implications for today can be argued out (e.g. agricultural prices, fishing problems, vinegar on chips). Behind these squabbles lies the big question, 'For the sake of unity and peace should we give up some of our sovereignty?'. Discussed in this practical context the concept of sovereignty can take on some concrete reality.

ACTIVITIES
Construction: a map of the members of the EEC showing the location of its various institutions
Compilation: a newspaper cutting book of EEC affairs
Television programme: preparing a series on member states of the EEC
Reports: on the proceedings of the European Parliament
Debates: on current issues from both the British and continental viewpoints
Writing: an essay on the question, 'Is full sovereignty necessary for Britain or for any nation?'

BOOKS FOR THE PUPIL
Current newspaper or magazine material and also:
Armitage, D., *The Common Market*, Macdonald.

Davies, M., *Europe Around Us*, Holmes McDougall.
Robottom, J. (ed.), *Making the Modern World – Europe*, Longman.
Savage, K., *The History of the Common Market*, Kestrel Books.
Thomas, M. W., *Focus on the E.E.C.*, In Focus, Nelson.

AUDIO-VISUAL MATERIALS
The Common Market, K. Brask and I. Bass, Education Audio-Visual. 2
colour filmstrips with notes and cassette.

4.2 Experiences of difference

4.2.1 *Introduction to the experience of some great leaders of thought*
At this stage standing in other people's shoes can be interpreted in
terms of thought and feeling as well as action. The following
suggestions are made with the idea that in each case there is a
background very different from ours, yet with fundamental common
elements of experience which make the characters intelligible.
Obviously there is room for a quite different selection.
i. *Socrates* A great and wise individualist whom the petty democrats
of Athens feared and therefore attacked. The story of his defence and
then acceptance of his condemnation, as told by Plato, raises many
fundamental questions that concern us today: the freedom of the
individual, how far the state can allow free criticism, just or unjust
trial, accepting a verdict whether just or unjust, the power to die.
ii. *St Augustine* Living in an age when the Roman Empire, which
people thought would endure to the end of time, was crashing round
their ears, when new barbarian people seemed to be roaming
everywhere, when society was changing rapidly and everyone felt
insecure. In this situation St Augustine, a North African bishop,
sought to strengthen his people, help refugees and proclaim that in
the midst of chaos there is an enduring society, the City of God.
iii. *St Francis* Another great individualist who reacted against
thirteenth-century material wealth by stripping off his rich clothes
and 'marrying' the Lady Poverty. The stories of his many adventures
show vividly what happens when someone carries his convictions to
their logical limits.
iv. *Dante* A poet whose Lady, Beatrice, died young, who backed the
wrong party in politics and was exiled, and who spent the rest of his
days wandering impotently from patron to patron, yet produced a
great vision of the Rule of Love which activated and governed the
whole universe, and showed what human society might be like if
people grasped this vision.

v. *Martin Luther*   The reformer whose convictions sprang from a deep religious experience and who was carried forward step by step to oppose the church hierarchy and finally to lead the Reformation.

vi. *Sir Thomas More*   A kind, clever, witty scholar who wanted a better and more reasonable society but fell into the clutches of an unreasonable king and was executed because he was faithful to his religious principles.

vii. *Voltaire*   The great rationalist of the eighteenth century who hated superstition and bigotry and wanted to destroy beliefs which could not be proved by reason.

viii. *Marx*   The researcher in the British Museum who, by studying past economic and social change, showed how societies could be changed today and sparked off revolutions.

Other possibilities: Confucius, Mohammed, Chairman Mao.

ACTIVITIES

Source work: discussion of extracts from the writings or sayings of
    thinkers in order to enter into and respond to their thoughts

Compilation of a 'Book of Thinkers': with pictures, biographies, extracts
    from writings and essays on why these people are interesting or
    important

Dramatisation: the stories of Socrates, St Augustine, St Francis and
    Luther particularly lend themselves to this

Discussion: on the moral issues involved, how far these people were
    successes or failures, whether we judge them to be 'great'

BOOKS

For the pupil

Amey, P., *Luther, Erasmus and Loyola*, Harrap.

Barker, D. R., *Story of Ancient Athens*, Arnold.

Cubitt, H., *Luther and the Reformation*, Then and There, Longman.

Devonshire Jones, R., *Erasmus and Luther*, Clarendon Biographies,
    Oxford University Press.

Evans, R., *Socialism*, Hamish Hamilton.

Green, R. L., *Ancient Greece*, Weidenfeld & Nicolson.

Painter, D., *Mao Tse-tung*, Harrap.

Ritchie, W. K., *The Eighteenth-Century Grand Tour*, Then and There,
    Longman.

Sheppard, E. J., *Ancient Athens*, Then and There, Longman.

For the teacher

Any translation of Plato's Socratic dialogues, especially the *Phaedo*.

Any translation of St Augustine's *Confessions*.

Any edition of Sir Thomas More's *Utopia*.
Bolt, R., *A Man for All Seasons*, Heinemann.
Brown, P., *Augustine of Hippo*, Faber.
Sayers, D. L., *The Divine Comedy* (translated), Penguin.
Sayers, D. L., *Further Papers on Dante*, Methuen.

AUDIO-VISUAL MATERIAL
Martin Luther, E. R. Chamberlin, Jackdaw no. 69, Jackdaw
   Publications.

4.2.2 *Some great 'moments' in European and world history*
Obviously not all the topics listed below could be covered. It is
important to take a topic in depth, with full background detail rather
than to touch many superficially. Activities are listed at the end of the
section and the relevant books appear under each topic heading.
i. *Renaissance and Reformation*   The literary aspects of the Renaissance
do not carry as much appeal as the beauty of art and architecture and
the drive of curiosity about the natural world which are well summed
up in Leonardo da Vinci whose career could be followed in detail. The
richness of the Italian Renaissance scene can most easily be studied in
Florence. New ideas on religion – as represented in Erasmus, Luther,
Calvin – lead on to the Reformation Churches. Emphasis can be
placed on (a) the specific beliefs for which people would die and
(b) the kind of social communities these new churches formed. St
Ignatius Loyola is probably the best example to take from the
Catholic side.

BOOKS FOR THE PUPIL
Amey, P., *Luther, Erasmus and Loyola*, Harrap.
Ball, G., *The Renaissance*, Hart-Davis.
Chamberlin, E., *Florence in the Time of the Medici*, Then and There,
   Longman.
Cowie, L., *The Reformation*, Hart-Davis.
Cowie, L., *The Reformation*, Wayland.
Cubitt, H., *Luther and the Reformation*, Then and There, Longman.
Francis, F. B. K., *Leonardo da Vinci*, Hutchinson.
Grant, N., *The Renaissance*, Franklin Watts.
Jones, R. D., *Erasmus and Luther*, Clarendon Biographies, Oxford
   University Press.
Richards, V. C., *Life and Times of Michelangelo*, Portraits of Greatness,
   Hamlyn.
Thomas, J., *Leonardo da Vinci*, Muller.
Williams, J., *Leonardo da Vinci*, Cassell Caravel.

AUDIO-VISUAL MATERIAL

Rome – the eternal city: part IV: the Renaissance, Time Life. Colour filmstrip with notes.

The Protestant Reformation, Education Audio-Visual. 2 colour filmstrips with notes and cassette.

John Knox and the Reformation in Scotland, Church of Scotland. Black and white filmstrip with notes.

Florence in the Time of the Medici, M. Reeves, Longman/Common Ground. 12 colour slides with notes.

Leonardo da Vinci (1452–1519), Slide Centre. 8 colour slides with notes. (The Slide Centre catalogue contains slide sets on a wide range of Renaissance artists.)

Michelangelo, BBC Radiovision. Colour filmstrip with notes to accompany radio broadcast in 'Religion and Life' series.

The Renaissance, H. Cubitt, Longman/Common Ground. 3 colour filmstrips with notes.

ii. *The Scientific Revolution of the sixteenth and seventeenth centuries*   New exploration of the natural world leads to new discoveries and ideas as represented by Copernicus, Galileo, Harvey, Boyle, Newton. The new idea of harnessing natural resources to the service of mankind was proclaimed by Sir Francis Bacon and in the seventeenth century the Royal society brought together in England an enthusiastic group of curious men.

BOOKS FOR THE PUPIL

Amey, P., *The Scientific Revolution*, Harrap.

Clash, P., *Famous Names in Science*, Wayland.

Gordon, S., *A Pageant of Scientists*, Blackwell.

North, J., *Isaac Newton*, Clarendon Biographies, Oxford University Press.

Walton, J., *Six Physicists*, Oxford University Press.

Wymer, N., *Medical Scientists and Doctors*, Oxford University Press.

Famous Scientists, Macdonald Junior Reference Library, Macdonald.

AUDIO-VISUAL MATERIAL

Newton and Gravitation, C. Ronan, Jackdaw no. 82. Jackdaw Publications.

Harvey and the Circulation of the Blood, J. Miller, Jackdaw no. 87, Jackdaw Publications.

William Harvey, Encyclopaedia Britannica. Colour filmstrip with captions.

iii. *The great days of Spain and the Revolt of the Netherlands*   The grandeur and tragic weaknesses of sixteenth-century Spain can be set against her social background and understood imaginatively by juxtaposing the richness of her art and literature and the great achievement of her empire to the pathetic weaknesses of Philip II and her poverty and economic decline. Over against this picture stands that of the up-and-coming Netherlands, the industry, trade and culture of the people and their heroic stand against Spain. This story is full of drama. The topic offers a good opportunity to practise trying to understand two sides with sympathy.

BOOKS FOR THE PUPIL

Cubitt, H., *Holland in the Time of Rembrandt*, Then and There, Longman.

Cubitt, H., *Spain and her Empire under Philip II*, Then and There, Longman.

de Iongh, H., *William the Silent and the Dutch Revolt*, Then and There, Longman.

Dorner, J., *Cortes and the Aztecs*, Then and There, Longman.

Fisher, J. R., *Latin America*, Hart-Davis.

Mackinnon, C., *Philip II; William the Silent*, Stories of Courage, Oxford Children's Reference Library, Oxford University Press.

Tate, E. N., *Pizarro and the Incas*, Then and There, Longman.

Weggelaer, J., *Amsterdam*, Famous Cities, Chambers.

AUDIO-VISUAL MATERIAL

Spain in the time of Philip II, H. Cubitt, Longman/Common Ground. 12 colour slides with notes.

Velazquez, Educational Productions. Colour filmstrip with notes.

Rembrandt Harmenszoon van Rijn (1606–1669), Slide Centre. 8 colour slides with notes.

Cortes and the Aztecs, J. Dorner, Longman/Common Ground. 12 colour slides with notes.

iv. *Louis XIV – 'Le Roi Soleil'*   Here again is a picture of brilliance and weakness symbolised in the King himself. The culture of his court and the glory of Versailles must be juxtaposed to the poverty and crushing tax burdens of the people, his grand concept of monarchy to his overweening ambition which finally crippled France. Social life and culture are more important here than a detailed account of Louis's wars.

BOOKS FOR THE PUPIL
Apsler, A., *The Sun King, Louis XIV of France*, Julian Messner.
Ritchie, W. K., *The France of Louis XIV*, Then and There, Longman.

AUDIO-VISUAL MATERIAL
France in the time of Louis XIV, W. K. Ritchie, Longman/Common
   Ground. 12 colour slides with notes.
Versailles, BBC Radiovision. Colour filmstrip with notes to
   accompany radio broadcast in 'World History' series.

v. *The French Revolution*   Again, it is important to spend a good deal of
time on the social background and grievances of all classes of people
and to follow in detail the opening stages of the revolution, rather than
to tease out the later politics. Certain dramatic scenes easily catch the
imagination, e.g. the storming of the Bastille, the women's march to
Versailles to fetch the royal family, the attempt of the royal family to
escape, and scenes from the careers of leaders such as Robespierre.
For discussion there are the great issues of whether violence gets you
what you want, whether it was necessary to execute the King and
Queen, whether power corrupted the revolutionary leaders and
whether it always does.

BOOKS FOR THE PUPIL
Rosenthal, M., *The French Revolution*, Then and There, Longman.

AUDIO-VISUAL MATERIAL
The French Revolution, Education Audio-Visual. 2 colour filmstrips
   with notes and cassette.
The French Revolution, rev. edn, R. Lacey, Jackdaw no. 147, Jackdaw
   Publications.

vi. *Napoleon*   Here, of course, the emphasis will be fairly and squarely
on a man, one of the giants of European history. To get inside this
topic imaginatively it is more important to follow Napoleon's
personal life and feelings and to understand how his soldiers lived and
why they adored him than to trace out his diplomacy and campaigns
in conscientious detail, though, of course, some highlights such as the
Moscow adventure and the strategy of Waterloo are fascinating to do
in detail. For discussion, clearly, the whole question of what makes a
'hero' comes up: must he believe in himself absolutely and seek
absolute power, and when and how does his ambition let him down?
These three French topics (iv, v, vi) together raise the question of
whether, for success, a nation must have one great leader and what
are the dangers of this.

BOOKS FOR THE PUPIL
Cammiade, A., *Napoleon*, Methuen.
Cooper, L., *The Young Napoleon*, Max Parrish.
Holden, M., *Napoleon in Russia*, Wayland.
Hutt, M., *Napoleon*, Clarendon Biographies, Oxford University Press.
Musman, R., *Napoleon*, Hutchinson.
Pratt, S., *Napoleon*, Wayland.
Richardson, P., *Nelson's Navy*, Then and There, Longman.
Speed, P. F., *Wellington's Army*, Then and There, Longman.
Sylvester, D., *Napoleon and the French Empire*, Then and There, Longman.
Tames, R. L. A., *Napoleon*, Harrap.

AUDIO-VISUAL MATERIAL
Europe at the time of Napoleon, 1812, Philip. Denoyer-Geppart Social Science Map.
The rise of Napoleon, R. Lacey, Jackdaw no. 71, Jackdaw Publications.
Napoleon, S. M. Newton, Visual Publications. 2 colour filmstrip with notes.

vii. *Garibaldi and the Italian Risorgimento*   Again a great story of a heroic bid for national freedom which can be told in dramatic detail. Of course, the complex politics of the Italian situation and the various forces within it, making for and against national independence, must be studied, but the main focus can be on the Garibaldi story.

BOOKS FOR THE PUPIL
Cooper, L., *Garibaldi*, Methuen.
Leeds, C., *The Unification of Italy*, Wayland.

AUDIO-VISUAL MATERIAL
Garibaldi and the Risorgimento, R. L. A. Tames, Jackdaw no. 74, Jackdaw Publications.

viii. *Russia in Europe*   A topic which falls into two parts: (a) focused on the personality and work of Peter the Great, casting back to medieval Russia (b) focused on the last Tsar and the Russian Revolution with Lenin and Stalin in the front of the picture. There are dramatic stories in both parts and a fascinatingly different background of the country and its people to be explored. In discussion the French and Russian Revolutions can be compared and the whole question of achieving social, economic and political reforms through forceable, even violent, methods can be debated.

BOOKS FOR THE PUPIL
Cubitt, H., *Russia under the Last Tsar*, Then and There, Longman.
Gibson, M., *Peter the Great*, Wayland.
Kennett, J., *The Growth of Modern Russia*, Blackie.
Killingray, D., *The Russian Revolution*, Harrap.
Kochan, L., *Lenin*, Hart-Davis.
Kochan, L., *Russian Revolution*, Pictorial Sources, Wayland.
Mack, D., *Lenin and the Russian Revolution*, Then and There, Longman.
Ritchie, W. K., *Russia under Peter the Great*, Then and There, Longman.
Roberts, E. M., *Lenin and the Downfall of Tsarist Russia*, Methuen.
Pickering, S., *Twentieth-Century Russia*, Oxford University Press.

AUDIO-VISUAL MATERIAL
An Introduction to Russia in the Twentieth Century; part 1: Russia 1900–1928,
    Nicholas Hunter. 25 colour slides with notes.
History of Russia: part 3: The End of Tsarism 1857–1917,
    Longman/Common Ground. Black and white filmstrip with notes.
Revolution in Russia, BBC TV. Black and white filmstrip with notes.
Lenin, Anthony Cash, Jackdaw no. 113, Jackdaw Publications.
The Russian Revolution, Anthony Cash, Jackdaw no. 42, Jackdaw
    Publications.
Russian Revolution, Education Audio-Visual. 2 filmstrips with notes
    and cassette.

ix. *Frontiersmen and democracy in the United States*   The story of the
nineteenth-century tide of immigrants as it rolled across the vast
expanses of North America, the fate of the Indian tribes caught in its
passage, the struggles of the young American democracy to cope with
the problem of ruling these great territories, the sharpest issue of
slavery and the sharpest crisis of the Civil War. Finally, the issue of
how federal government works can be studied and debated, and its
problems contrasted with those of a government like Britain's.

BOOKS FOR THE PUPIL
Allt, A., *The American Civil War*, Then and There, Longman.
Cammiade, A., *Lincoln and the American Civil War*, Methuen.
Campbell, A. B., *Homesteaders and Indians*, Franklin Watts.
Campbell, A. B., *North American Indians*, Muller.
Clarke, C., *The Young American Republic*, Then and There, Longman.
Currie, B., *Gold Miners in the American West*, Then and There,
    Longman.
Currie, B., *Pioneers in the American West 1780–1840*, Then and There,
    Longman.

Currie, B., *Railroads and Cowboys in the American West*, Then and There, Longman.
Gray, L. L., *How We Choose a President*, St Martin's Press.
Hoare, R. J., *Cowboys and Cattle Trails*, Hulton.
Huggett, F. E., *Slaves and Slavery*, Lutterworth Press.
Lester, J., *To Be A Slave*, Puffin Books.
Taylor, G., *The American South before the Civil War*, Then and There, Longman.
Ullyatt, K., *The Time of the Indian*; *The Day of the Cowboy*, Kestrel Books.

AUDIO-VISUAL MATERIAL
The American Civil War (1861–1865), Rickitt. 18 slides with notes.
Slavery and the Civil War, B. Beacroft, Longman/Common Ground. Colour filmstrip with notes.
Lincoln frees the slaves, BBC Radiovision. 2 black and white filmstrips with notes to accompany radio broadcast.
The American Civil War, D. Johnson, Jackdaw no. 106, Jackdaw Publications.
The 'Grapes of Wrath' and the 1930s, Education Audio-Visual. 2 black and white filmstrips with notes and cassette.

x. *Contrasts of the two world wars*   A full treatment of causes and strategies in the two wars would form a subject still extremely complex at this stage, but causes can be approached in the simpler way through personalities, e.g. the Kaiser, Hitler, Mussolini; and strategies can be studied through contrasts in the weapons and machines of the two wars and the personal experiences of those who fought, e.g. the contrast between trench warfare and that of the 'desert rats'. Particular episodes can be highlighted, e.g. the tragic Gallipoli expedition in the First World War and the siege of Malta in the Second World War, or the War in the Far East. There is a wealth of personal reminiscence to be used. Discussion might focus, *inter alia*, on the paradox between the exhilarating heroism and self-sacrificing comradeship experienced in warfare and its brutality, callousness and basically destructive purpose.

BOOKS FOR THE PUPIL
Borer, M. C., *The First World War*, Macmillan.
Case, S. L., *The First World War*, Evans.
Catchpole, B., *Twentieth-Century Germany*, Oxford University Press.
Edwards, T., *D-Day*, Wayland.
Gibbons, S. R. and Morican, P., *World War One*, Modern Times, Longman.

Gray, P., *D. Day*, McGraw Hill.

Healey, T., *The Second World War*, Macdonald.

Heater, D., *The Cold War*, The Changing World, Oxford University Press.

Hobbs, A., *Battle of Britain*, Wayland.

Holden, M., *Desert Rats*, Wayland.

Holden, M., *Hitler*, Wayland.

Holland, P., *Twentieth-Century France*, Oxford University Press.

Leeds, C., *Italy under Mussolini*, Wayland.

Parkinson, R., *Origins of World War One*, Wayland.

Parkinson, R., *Origins of World War Two*, Wayland.

Peacock, R., *The Second World War*, Macmillan.

Savage, K., *A State of War – Europe 1939–1945*, Oxford University Press.

Savage, K., *The Story of the Second World War*, Oxford University Press.

Sellman, R. R., *The First World War*, Methuen.

Williams, J., *Gallipoli*, Lutterworth Press.

Yass, M., *The Home Front*, Wayland.

AUDIO-VISUAL MATERIAL

In the Trenches, BBC Radiovision. 2 black and white filmstrips with notes to accompany radio broadcast.

The First World War, W. F. Norton, Longman/Common Ground. Black and white filmstrip with notes.

The First World War, J. Ray, History Broadsheets, Heinemann. 19 leaflets in folder.

First World War, D. Scotland, Exploring History Kit, Macmillan.

Newspapers of the First World War. I. Williams, David & Charles. Reprints.

Causes of World War I, Education Audio-Visual. 2 colour filmstrips with notes and cassette.

Assassination at Sarajevo, S. Nickels, Jackdaw no. 37, Jackdaw Publications.

Civilians in the two world wars, Rickitt. 24 slides with notes.

World War I 1914–1918: Eastern fronts, Rickitt. 12 black and white slides with notes.

The Somme 1916, R. L. A. Tames, Jackdaw no. 111, Jackdaw Publications.

The Western Front 1914–1918, M. Brice, HMSO. Photographs from Imperial War Museum.

The Second World War, W. F. Norton, Longman/Common Ground. Set of 2 black and white filmstrips with notes.

The summer of '45: a scrapbook, BBC. Cassette.

The voice of Winston Churchill, Decca. Cassette (KSXC 6200).

Causes of World War II, Education Audio-Visual. Colour filmstrip with notes and cassette.
The Battle of Britain, A. Burton (a dramatised documentary), Ivan Berg. Cassette (GE003).
Battle of Britain, B. Collier, Jackdaw no. 65, Jackdaw Publications.
Dunkirk, B. Collier, Jackdaw no. 130, Jackdaw Publications.
Britain at War, A. Calder, Jackdaw no. 66, Jackdaw Publications.

xi. *The Chinese Revolution*   This can be linked with previous work on Chinese civilisation and with the Second World War in the Far East. The weaknesses of old China and its outworn government will be placed in contrast to the revolutionary thought and achievements of Chairman Mao. For the transition there are personal writings such as those of Han Suyin. Discussion will centre on what has been achieved at what price and whether the discipline and absence of personal freedom in the present regime are acceptable.

BOOKS FOR THE PUPIL
Goldston, R., *The Long March*, Franklin Watts.
Painter, D., *Mao Tse-tung*, Harrap.
Roberts, E. M., *Mao Tse-tung and the Chinese Communist Revolution*, Methuen.
Spencer, C., *Modern China*, Hart-Davis.
Weston, A., *The Chinese Revolution*, Harrap.

AUDIO-VISUAL MATERIAL
Revolution in China: 1911–1949, History Broadsheets, Heinemann. 21 leaflets in folder.
China: society in change since 1900, J. Robottom, Longman/Common Ground. Colour filmstrip with notes.
Revolution in China, BBC TV. Black and white filmstrip with notes.
The People's Republic of China, History Broadsheets, Heinemann. 26 leaflets in folder.

ACTIVITIES
See topics i–xi above
Individual assignments: on geographical background, personalities, special aspects, as appropriate
Maps and charts: relating to the topics, as appropriate
Compilation: of a 'period book', or picture, or filmstrip, or television programme on the social and cultural backgrounds in, e.g. topics i, iii, iv, v, vi, viii, ix, xi
Critical study: and discussion of source material, how 'true' is it?

Composition: of biographies of leading characters, with illustrations and quotations from their sayings or writings

Dramatisation of scenes: e.g. St Francis on the road, Luther before the Diet of Worms, Galileo before the Inquisition, scenes from the Revolt of the Netherlands or French Revolution, American frontiersmen

Imaginative and argumentative writing: (a) contemporary newspapers or posters illustrating, e.g. topics iii, v, vi, vii, viii, ix, xi. (b) imaginary letters, diaries, speeches, as appropriate

Mounting an exhibition: to give concrete meaning to one or more of the commonly used terms: Renaissance, Reformation, Scientific Revolution, Louis Quatorze, Napoleonic France, Totalitarianism

Debates and discussions: on questions as suggested under each topic

4.3 Threads or themes

These may well suit the mood better than the period pieces suggested above, especially as they can often be successfully pursued as individual projects. The following are only suggestions.

4.3.1 *History of medicine, surgery and hospitals*
Galen and Hippocrates; medieval medicine; development of surgery (related to warfare); Harvey; nineteenth- and twentieth-century advances.

4.3.2 *Human rights*
From serfdom to personal freedom; from suppression of freedom of thought to toleration; from persecution of minority groups to political freedom; from the tyranny of law to rights before the law; culminating in today's Human Rights Charter and its continuing abuse (Amnesty International, etc.).

4.3.3 *Development of power and energy*
From human muscle force to atomic power: a study to be linked with science and leading to a consideration of whether we are abusing our resources in natural energy.

4.3.4 *The hero in history and literature*
A theme which allows very wide choice of examples in different periods and culminates in the question 'What makes a hero?'.

4.3.5 *Enthusiasm/fanaticism in history*
Bringing together examples from different periods and looking for answers to such questions as 'What is enthusiasm?' 'What makes

people enthusiastic?' 'What is the difference between the enthusiastic person and the fanatical person?' 'How important have such people been in history?' Possible examples are Alexander the Great, St Paul and other early Christians, early followers of Mohammed, the People's Crusade, the Children's Crusade, St Francis, Lollard heretics, St Francis Xavier, seventeenth-century Radicals (Ranters, Levellers, etc.), some leaders in the French Revolution, Napoleon, some modern totalitarian leaders, Suffragettes, Martin Luther-King.

ACTIVITIES

These could include all types previously mentioned, but if a long time-span is covered, the first essential is a time-chart.

BOOKS

See previous book-lists.

Finally, at this stage, or earlier in the secondary school, a theme on *What is History?* can be very rewarding, starting with the difference between pre-history and history, and going on to study how and why people started recording their doings, what types of records they evolved, the differences between chronicles, diaries, letters and official documents, the uses and dangers of eye-witness history, the value of visual sources and their limitations, and how we test reliability in sources. In the early stages, concrete examples of types of record (e.g. inscriptions, writs, tally-sticks, pipe-rolls, chronicles, etc.) need to be used; later, different accounts of the same happening can be compared for discrepancies and some forgeries can be studied. The topic could culminate in the problems of writing twentieth-century history: how soon after events can reliable history be written; can personal memoirs be used, how soon should government offices open their documents to the public?

Index

Italics refer to a topic within a suggested syllabus (Chapter 8).